ANGEL IN THE COURTROOM

My story of surviving the injustice of incarceration

Contents of Book

1. Love comes softly……………………………………..page 1-9
2. Reconnecting with Kerry……………………………..page 10-22
3. The Big Fall…………………………………………..page 23-34
4. The Arrest and Booking……………………………...page 35-39
5. Adapting to Jail……………………………………… page 40-50
6. The Trial……………………………………………… page 51-55
7. The prosecution version/my facts…………………… page 56-62
8. Saving my grandson "Keshawn"…………………….. page 63-70
9. Family/friends and my faith – The 3-F's……………page 71-84
10. And, so my journey begins in Prison………………..page 85-97
11. All is revealed………………………………………..page 98-111
12. The Waiting Game…………………………………..page 112-117
13. The Hearing…………………………………………..page 118-126
14. Decision Time………………………………………..page 127-134
15. Mankind vs. God……………………………………..page 135-140
16. Resting in God's Promises/on Seeking God………..page 141-145
17. Amazing Grace (My chains are gone)……………….page 146-151
18. Starting Over…………………………………………page 152-156
19. Angel in the Courtroom ……………………………..page 157-160
20. Songs that got me through my time………………… page 161-164
21. Poems…………………………………………………page 165-172

I dedicate this book to my grandson Keshawn Jones

Acknowledgements:

I want to give a million thanks to Ms. Bell, Ms. Blount, Ms. Hunter, Denise H., Roger .and David, who all stood by my side faithfully from day one encouraging me as I passed through the fire of oppression. Each one of these people have had a positive impact in my life. You guys are the bomb!!! They all also not knowing performed the roles of good spiritual mentors.

To my grandson: Keshawn Jones, whom visited his grandma diligently, and my sister, "Jacqueline Carr," that knows how to keep a promise, in bringing him each time and for typing on this entire manuscript for me. I love you guys.

Psalms 35:27 – Let them shout for joy and be glad who favored my righteous cause.

Thank you Jesus so very much for giving your angels orders concerning me and for letting my enemies see your wondrous works and putting them to shame, because you Lord have helped and comforted me. May the Lord be praised for he has heard the sound of my pleading (Psalm 20:6). Now I know that the Lord gives victory to his anointed.

A million Thanks to my Attorney, Mrs. Kittay, who never knew that me and my sister both had prayed to the father, asking him to pour his anointment unto her, on my behalf and use her for my victory. She opened the door for me to get me back into the courts, with powerful briefs each time.

I also would like to give a heartily shout-out to all the women in Hazelton prison, who knew me during my time spent there.

Additionally, I want to send out a grand Thank You to two powerful prayer warriors, Elder Jeffrey Rustin and Minister Elaine Robinson, at our church, because they each knew my story and stood in the gap with my sister Jacqueline, praying me back home. (Matthew 18:20)

1 Thessalonians 5:18: "In everything, give thanks, for this is the will of God in Christ Jesus concerning you."

(KJV)

Confessions:

I felt the need to write this book, so no one could accuse me of hoarding secrets, not that I need other people's validation of me, only God's, but nor can they accuse me of lying about my past. No one can say that I pretended to be something that I wasn't or better than the next person. I have tried to the best of my ability to confess and disclose my past to my family and friends, who cared enough to listen. Being honest takes many armaments out of the enemy's arsenal. As a result, I can breathe easier and sleep better at night. I have nothing to hide. I don't carry guilt. My load is gone, because I have come clean. But, it's ok, if they still want to scandalize my name, because I'm bound now for the promise land and I'll never let go of his hand again. So, if anyone chooses to judge me for taking a life, he or she will have to stand before God in judgment and give an account for his or her actions. The gossiper will be revealed as exactly what they are, an instrument of Satan. Ecclesiastes 7:20 tells us, for there is not a just man on earth who does good and does not sin.

A very important lesson stands out from this experience. If you do the crime/break the law, you must stand ready to do the time. It is important to reach out in honesty and be real about who you are, then people will respect you more for it. When we share our brokenness it also strengthens our faith.

Yes, what I have done will definitely be with me for the rest of my life….. It will continually be before me and I will be sorry for this sin forever.

Intro

I gathered my things together and locked the building up. Since there was no traffic that time of night, I was home in about fifteen minutes. Once I turned onto my street "Tubman Road", I saw a policeman car sitting there, so I slowed down, as "I approached the stop sign"… Then proceeded around the block, into the alley of my driveway and parked. By the time I had gotten there, I could see "Kerry's" car parked in front of the house. Once I got out of my car and went into my house through the back door, he was coming through the front door with my grandson, not saying a word or anything. So I proceeded upstairs, so I could get my grandson dressed and bring him back to work with me, until I got off from work later that morning.

Once I got my grandson's clothes and coat on, and was prepared to leave back out, it bothered me that "Kerry," still was not saying a word to me, by then he was in the bathroom, brushing his teeth, so I approached him, asking him, what kind of man are you without a "heart and soul" to leave a little boy in the house alone, this time of night.

He finishes brushing his teeth, then comes up to me fast, pointing his finger in my face, yelling and saying, "I knew it, I knew it," just knew you were going to blame me for this "shit." I said, well who else I am supposed to blame, I left you in the house with him. "No," he said, you should be blaming your "Bitch Ass" daughter. Then he surprisingly lifted me up, threw me onto our bed, slammed me face down and continued jerking me up and down by my collar, yelling at me like a crazy man, gone mad. I was yelling out to him to "stop it," and to "get off of me," then he yanked me up, still by the back of my collar, and then threw me up against the wall, still yelling like a mad man. At this point, my grandson is crying and scared. He tells me at some point, that he will take me out of my misery and to stay here. I say, I'm calling the police right now, he says, by the time they get here, you will be dead, "Bitch." I'm going to end this "shit" tonight! Then he ran down the stairs to the 1st level.

The first thing I thought was, oh my God, I'm going to die!

Now I am in a panic, not knowing what he will do or thinking of for sure, so I run upstairs, my grandson in pursuit behind me. Once I reached the top landing, I go into my closet, where I knew I hid my "38" and load a bullet into the chamber. I then placed it into my waistband, hiding it with my long winter coat. I then paced the floor, hoping that he would perhaps just leave the house and go somewhere to cool off. But then I suddenly heard him coming back up the stairs fast, yelling again and cursing, as he got to the top of the landing. I could see the rage in his face. He then grabbed a pair of "6" inch green scissors that was on the desk caddy, he tempted to approach me, while pointing to my closet and screaming at me, asking "what color dress do you want to be buried in"? I was frozen and lost for words and something inside me just told me this is it "Moe," it's either you or him. I feared for my life and that of my then 5-year old grandson, that was standing beside me the entire time, and reached for the "38", as he was coming towards me, and I fired one shot, without knowing or realizing where I had hit him.

Instantly, he dropped the scissors and reached for the phone that was on the desk also, in an attempt to call 9-1-1, that's when he collapsed and blood started spurting from his mouth.

Ecclesiastes 3:1 – "A time and a season for Everything"

CHAPTER 1
Love comes softly

I still remember the day vividly. It was a hot day in July 1998. I was sitting on a park bench, taking a break between writing tickets, for the Dept. of Public Works, in "Georgetown Park" along the C&O canal.

Then along comes this tall, handsome, red-bone, charming man. I had noticed him on a couple of other occasions, strolling by, but on this particular day, he talked and flirted with me. We engaged into a long drawn out conversation. It went into my lunch break, so I remember asking him, did he mind having lunch with me and he happily said "sure", I would. Oh, but before him agreeing to have lunch with me, this charming man, introduced himself as "Kerry."

We walked up the street to the "subway" shop on the corner of "M" Street. He didn't expect for me to tell him, "don't worry, I got this." He told me, while eating he never had a woman to pay the tab, and I said, "oh well, first time for everything, right?" Little did we both know this would become our first date. During our meal, we both exchanged phone numbers. I had to return to work, so we departed and went our separate ways.

It would be a couple of days later, I received my first phone call from him. We both laughed and talked for hours on the phone, for several more weeks, before setting a date and time to meet again. Since neither of us drove at that time, and also lived on opposite sides of town, is probably what extended our meeting.

I eventually purchased a new/used "GT Mustang," burgundy and so pretty, but later I learned this car was a big gas guzzler. Every three days, I was re-filling it up again. At this time, I had two young daughters I had to get back and forth to my mom's house, who was the babysitter, and to work, which both were in DC and I lived in Forestville, MD.

After purchasing this vehicle, Kerry and I, eventually planned our first meeting, but he had no idea, what type of car I had purchased, so when I pulled up in front of him in this "bad and hot" GT-Mustang, he had to do a double take, looking inside, to ensure the right person he was waiting for was behind that wheel.

He was like "Wow", you really out-did yourself, didn't you? We both had to laugh on that one. This would be the first time, he would meet my two young daughters that were in the back seat. We all went out to eat at a nice restaurant, then I took him pass my apartment to see where I lived. Afterwards I got him back home safely.

It wasn't for long, we eventually started dating, and we hit it off quickly, sharing so much in common. About four months later, he moved in with me and the girls and from there our relationship took off.

We were like any average middle-class couple, we both worked, although I made the most income. We split all the bills down the middle. We did a lot of things together, like doing grocery and personal shopping. We would go to the Laundromat every week, out to eat occasionally and different little outings.

We both were neat, clean and organized individuals when it came down to keeping the place clean, so we were fortunate in that area. Occasionally, he would go along to church with us, but he wasn't too big on that, because he could never sit still long enough to hear the sermon through.

The thing I liked most about "Kerry," was that he was very romantic. Whatever opportunity he got as far as extra cash on his paycheck, he loved to buy me jewelry. He wanted me to have a ring for every finger, and nice necklaces. He also liked to flaunt wearing jewelry, especially watches.

"Kerry," never gave me any reason to suspect he was ever cheating on me, if he did, he hid it well. He would only make mention from time to time, that a couple of women had a crush on him, but he would tell them he only had eyes for me. I had no reason to cheat on him either, because I loved this man from the top of his head to the bottom of his feet and the ground he walked on. But there was one other man in the dark shadows of my life that could pop up anytime, and make me lose sight of the love I had for "Kerry." I believe this is when our love went down "south." My youngest daughter's father, "Hank," was just coming home from prison. Hank, would come out for a little while, then go back in for a minute. Call it crazy love, but there is something about a woman and her baby-daddy. There will always be a connection there or a spark. For some odd reason or another, whenever that man would resurface again, whomever I was with at the time, had nothing coming anymore.

Once fresh out of prison, he started calling regularly and eventually using the excuse of wanting to see his daughter. After this happened, Kerry wasn't having it, and I couldn't blame him. He wanted me to cut him completely out of my life, but I wasn't strong enough to do it.

So the arguments would soon start, the distrust and fighting all together. Although I never left Kerry to go with Hank, for some reason or another, our relationship just never seemed to get back to the good times again. It was like we both were always looking for reasons to despise one another. Since this was so long ago, to be honest with you, I can't even remember, what most of the arguing and fighting was about. It did happen, and when it happened, I saw "a man on fire."

"Kerry," felt like whatever me and him purchased together, had to be split up together. What I mean by this, is, say we had bought a T.V. together or a stereo, he would hold it up in the air and bring it down to the floor, splitting it into two, saying now there is your half and this is mine. I didn't like the fact also that he was an "Indian" giver. Whatever gifts he purchased for me, like all the jewelry I told you about earlier, he wanted them all back. Then when we smoothed things back over again, he would give them all back to me.

Another good quality about "Kerry," he was a good saver. He had saved up a thousand dollars to surprise me with, for what would be a down payment on me a brand new car. I bought a brand new 1999-Blue Dodge Neon that year.

We both took pleasure in driving to work, although it was in my name. So for several more months, we continued living together and making the best out of our relationship. "Kerry," was a good man, but he had a hidden dark-side. Behind closed doors, he reminded you of a coo-coo bird, sometimes this side of him would come out of nowhere, leaving me and the girls both puzzled. He would pace the floor back and forth, with his fist balled up and talking to himself.

    Between October and November of 1999, we had our last and final argument. Again, I can't even remember what the argument and fight was about this time. But it had gotten heated, with him storming out of the apartment, and telling me that the next time I saw my car, I wouldn't be able to recognize it. I yelled and screamed at him to not take my car anywhere and to give me my keys, but he kept going. I ran out of the apartment behind him, with my oldest daughter on my heels behind me. By the time I reached the parking lot, he was already in the car, ignition started and taking off, like Batman into the cold and nightly wind. I was so out-raged that I picked up a hand full of rocks and threw them as far as they would go, knowing darn well, he was too far gone, for one rock to hit that car.

    I ran back into the apartment and called the police to report my car stolen. They told me there wasn't anything they could do, since he lived there. I kept calling and ringing his phone, but he would never answer. The next morning, he had his best friend phone me, to tell me, where I could find the car.

He left it parked and abandoned on South Capitol Street, S.E. As I approached my car, I about passed out, I couldn't believe what I was seeing. It looked like a freight train had run into the entire driver's side of the car, windows were smashed in, and both doors. I then called for a tow truck to come and pick it up and tow it to the dealer.

I was so broken and torn into pieces, the next thing I did, was phone his probation officer. I told him what he had done. Then he asked me to send him pictures of the vehicle and a sworn affidavit of what had happened.

Once I did that, a warrant was immediately put out for his arrest. He phoned me a few days later, informing me he was turning himself in, and he probably would be gone away for a while. I then asked him why he do that to my car. He only could say he was sorry, and that being in love, sometimes makes you do the craziest things, and that I had made him just so "f" angry.

When the phone conversation ended, he told me he would phone me later, when he could, to let me know the outcome. Sure enough a few days later, he called to inform me that the parole board was recommending him to do eight years. "I was like, eight years for what", just vandalizing a car, he said, "No man, because of the fact, I violated my probation period." I asked him what exactly was his original charge? He told me it was for writing bad checks and credit card fraud. I replied, and said, you mean to tell me for that alone, you got to do eight more years. "Yeah man," he said, and I need you to recant your story and tell them you made a mistake. I was like "ok" give me the name and phone number of the person I need to talk with. I called, but a woman told me it was too late. Back then, I was so ignorant and dumb-founded to the laws, I didn't know the difference between a misdemeanor and a felony, and how much time one could get for any crime, so I believed him, when he told me about the eight years. But little did I know, I wound carry around that guilt and weight on my shoulders until he returned again.

After he went away, we remained in contact for about a year. I would visit him and send him money when I could. For that first year after his departure, I went to celebrate.

It wasn't long, after his departure that my life sort of took off rather fast. December of that same year, I started a new job with the Federal Government, working for the "Smithsonian" museums. In April of 2000, I was moving into my first owned condominium. It was gorgeous, 2 large bedrooms, 1-1/2 bathroom, a hot tub that was round-shaped, a nice sized dining and living room and oh the balcony was so unusual, it was a half of an oval circle-shaped, instead of the usual rectangle shape.

I still had the same Dodge Neon for about another year. I was fortunate that someone had stolen the Neon, and wrecked it so bad, until the insurance company paid it off. This left me with money over to put down on a brand new 2001 Ford Mustang that year. Later on, I got me a part-time night security job, to have extra income in my pockets.

While working at the "Smithsonian" museum, I met my next long-term partner, his name was "David." We dated for the first six months being celibate and taking our time getting to know one another. Our relationship lasted for almost five years, until I decided it was time for me to move and make a change. I resigned in 2004, sold my condominium and relocated to Atlanta, Georgia, where I resided for only a year. It was very difficult for me to find steady employment, paying me close to what I was making in DC. I was struggling and needed to move back.

A few months before moving back to DC, we lost my youngest daughter's father, "Hank." my daughter and I came back for a week for the funeral service and then back to Georgia for the next six months, until I made my official move back to DC.

Luckily, I still had "David" to lean on for support. He allowed me and my daughter to crash in with him, until I could get back on my feet and my own apartment again. This was in September 2005. I got my daughter back into school again, near his apartment. It wasn't long before I found me a part-time decent night-time job as a night-time receptionist in a Georgetown condominium. Within about three or four months, I was hired by a Security Company as a Security Guard. After this my future took off again, within a few months, I was promoted to supervisor, and in the early part of 2006, I was moving into my own apartment again.

My blessings were coming in fast. I was accepted for a full-time Security Guard position at the "National Gallery of Art." I had made it back into the Federal government in February 2007.

This time with the extra money I would make, I spent and saved it more wisely. I had no car note, still driving my Mustang that was in good running condition. I just kept up with the maintenance in place of not having that car note. I could save a portion of my money towards my new home, I was planning to purchase. Besides a settlement, I had already put money into a "CD" account.

Colossians 3:13 - Even as Christ forgave you, so you also must do.

CHAPTER II
RECONNECTING WITH "KERRY"

After being on the new job for about a month, I was getting settled in and meeting new friendly faces. Even to the point of hanging out with a couple guys after work for some fun and just kicking it, but it never led into sex, just simply platonic.

One morning while rushing to work, as I seldom did, in early April, as I got off of the train at "Archives," and reached to the top of the escalator, I happened to glance over to my right at the fare card machine, and noticed this tall, light-skinned man from behind, waiting in line to purchase a fare card. I said to myself, that man looks just like "Kerry," but then I tried to convince myself, "nah," it couldn't be. The only way I'm going to know for sure, is to go over there and stand near this person, so when he turns around and see me, our eyes can't help but lock onto one another. Sure enough that's what I did, and once he did turn around, I was like

"OMG" it really is you! He was in awe, saying "Moe," is that you? I can't believe it and he reached out his arms to hug me, then he said, I still can't believe, I ran into you. You still look good. How have you been? Are you married yet or in a relationship? I said "no," I'm not, at the moment. I never expected us to cross paths again.

Then I asked him, when he came home. He said he had only been out for a couple of weeks, and his probation officer had him out looking for jobs. I told him look, I'd love to finish talking to you, but if I don't leave now, I'm going to be late for work, and I'm pushing for the button right now. He asked if I had a phone number he could reach me on, I said sure I do, and reached into my purse for a pen and a piece of paper and wrote it down for him. Then he reached out again and hugged me good-bye.

I went home that afternoon from work, and told my youngest daughter, you would never believe who I ran into this morning going to work. She was like, who, I said "Kerry." She was not so thrilled at all, only saying, please don't tell me, you're going to hook up with that coo-coo bird again. I just laughed it off, without giving her any reassurance of a response.

Now, Kerry, didn't call me right away. It wasn't until about two weeks later when I heard from him. He told me, he was just getting out of the half-way house, and staying with his aunt in Oxon Hill, Maryland.

He went on to ask, when we could hook-up. So we set up a date and time for him to come over and see me at my apartment. It was like the chemistry between us, never departed. He started visiting more often and sometimes even spending the night, of course.

It never seemed to take Kerry long to find employment, even after just being released from prison. He had just started working for a construction company on the mid-night shift, off of New York Avenue. But, by him getting off work, such an odd time at 5 am in the morning, he and a co-worker friend of his had to wait around for a half hour until the metro station opened up.

So, after a few weeks of having done this, I offered him my car to drive, since by the time he went to work and got off, I wasn't driving it. By there being no traffic that time of morning, he would arrive back to my apartment in no time, with the metro train still not being opened yet. He would bring his co-worker over to crash on my sofa until the metro station opened up, and then he would get up and walk from my apartment to the station.

For about a year, I owned a timeshare in Williamsburg, VA. My usage to vacation in this timeshare was every year, the week of "Memorial Day." Already having my vacation plans and leave put in for this, way long before realizing that I would be reconnecting with "Kerry."

I invited him to come along with us, meaning myself, my youngest daughter, and my then 4-year old grandson. Luckily, by just coming home he was able to leave the city and come with us. I figured a vacation would be just what he needed, so he came along. Besides, who could refuse a free trip! (LOL).

We drove down for the entire week. We all had a ball, while the chemistry between us was still heating up and just getting started. After the vacation was over, we both decided we would date again. So we did just that for the next couple of months, before we both decided that we wanted to live together again. It was in August 2007, when he officially moved in with me.

The following month, September 12, 2007, we were exchanging wedding vows at the justice of peace. "Yes," things did move rather quickly between us and maybe it was because it wasn't like we had just met. We both had loved one another almost a decade earlier. So, at the time, it felt so right.

In spite of my insecurities, telling me "No," don't do it! First of all, I responded "we'll be fine." Secondly, my mind was being bombarded from every which way. I began to feel like I was in the middle of some tug-a-war contest. Do it! Don't do it! Do it! Back and forth it went. I finally ended the conflict.

"No," I didn't receive clear confirmation from the Lord, and the Bible says, when you try to pursue your own plans and not his, you will fail. Proverbs 19:21.

Kerry had convinced me as much as he could that he was a changed man, and he would never hurt me again. I was his soul mate and only destiny could have brought us back together again. He went on and on, elaborating on how much we were meant for one another.

The ceremony, which consisted of my daughter Ekia and her friend Erica. They were our witnesses, and our photographers. We later had reservations on the "Spirit of Washington" cruise ship. It wasn't anything extravagant, but romantic and served the purpose.

We decided we were not going to spend a lot of money on a reception, because I had already been in the process of house hunting and locking in on one in particular.

After a few months of me handling financial issues with the bank, lenders, and seminars on 1st time home buyers, I finally settled on a brand new home that was in the process of being built. It would be all of our dream home, and fresh new start.

In December 2007, we were moving in our new home. I'd hired professional movers and since they were on the clock, being paid by the hour, they were moving very slow. I remember Kerry, taking the initiative and helping with the move, to keep from going over an allotted budget we both had planned out. We were about saving a buck, but on the other hand, we could both tell by the look on the movers faces, they weren't too pleased. (LOL).

Only a few months into the marriage, the first encounter started with Kerry and my daughter "Tameka." An argument pursued between them and he ended up calling her a "B." I was at work this particular day when it happened. I got a call from my daughter, informing me that she was on her way down to my job, to tell me what happened. Once she got there, and started telling me her version of what happened, I believed her and assured her I would talk to him. Depending on the outcome, I was going to prepare to leave him, because I wasn't going to allow any man to talk to my daughter that way, let alone, call her the "B" word. She knew that I wouldn't even call her that word.

    Just so happen that while we were talking, I received a call over the radio that my husband, was on his way over to my location. Meka heard that, so she decided to leave before he approached. He wanted to tell me his version, but didn't deny calling her a "B." I reminded him of how important my daughter is to me, and if he didn't think he could get along with her, it was best we parted now. He promised me that it was never going to happen again, and he would apologize to her, as soon as he saw her. After he left, I called Tameka, and told her that he said, he was sorry, and he is going to apologize to you, so let's give him another chance. I don't think she wanted too, but for me, she did. Then things sort of went back to normal.

Now I am going to take you through a series of different episodes I went through with Kerry; all in the year of 2008. Not in this specific order, because I can't recall from memory, but at least every couple of months, I could expect something.

Life had started to get better for him, because he was later hired by Howard University Hospital as a maintenance worker that allotted him a stable salary and benefits. Then a couple of months later, he picked up a part-time job at "Bed, Bath & Beyond." He wanted to start saving so he could get his own car, since my car was the only car in the household.

On a couple of different occasions, he was the one behind the wheel, in my car, causing each minor collisions. Once the deductible went up the second time, I asked him to cover the difference. He did so for only two months, after that he refused to give anything else towards it.

Another explosion time for him came when I once assumed, and you know how the story goes about assuming. One of our many agreements was that, we each would buy groceries on the week we got paid, since that was on opposite weeks. So anyway, this particular day, he says to me, let's go to the grocery store, this is when it was only my car in the picture. Anyway, once we arrived there, got out of the car, and before going into the entrance of the store, I asked him, as I always did, how much we were spending, so we both could be adding up as we picked up things, and didn't go over our budget. Then he says to me, what do you mean, "How much we're spending." I then said to him, well it is your week for the shopping. He then says, well, "I ain't got no money". I then said, well why in the heck did you say let's go to the grocery store! He said, "Because I thought it was your turn to buy." I said,

"Why did you think that when it's not even my pay week, it's yours." So from there, we both went back and forth, making a scene, causing everyone to look at us, as they passed by. He started flicking off again, and once he does, he gives you no chance to be rational with him. I said, "ok, since we are already here, we might-as-well go inside, and I'll pay for it out of one of the bills." "You have to reimburse it back to me, soon as you get paid again." He says "Hell, then I'll be paying double in the same week." I go, "What will be the difference, when I'm paying twice now." He flat out says, the answer is "no," and "I am out of here, do what you want to, I will walk home."

He left me standing there looking like a fool and started walking. Now from where we were back to the house would probably had been like a 2-1/2 – 3 hour walk, verses like 15-20 minutes by car. I was so mad and smoking hot. I went on inside anyway and bought just a few things. Then instead of going straight back home, I made a couple of stops that took about 2 hours, and by the time I got home, he was already there. So I never knew whether he actually walked or how he got there.

I didn't ask, because normally it went like this whenever we both had one of these heated arguments. We'll go a couple of days without speaking.

Not long after I'd gotten home, his favorite cousin came over. I was upstairs watching T.V. when he brought her up there to say hello to me. He told her about what happened between the both of us earlier, and to get her opinion. To make a long story short, it became heated again, to the point of him, standing up, racing over to me, ready to knock my head off, until his cousin had to intervene and stop him. I got to admit, I was shaking like a leaf on a tree, so hard, trying to hide it.

I couldn't use this incident as another outrageous violent act, because, as you'll read about it later on in the book, I'd incriminate my own self, by writing about all this to the prosecutor, assuming he was on my side.

Another embarrassing and frightening time, was a Sunday morning, when me, him and my grandson were going to church. Before getting out of the car, he asked me, what time does the service end. I told him normally around 1 pm. So we all went into the church together and we were escorted to our seats. After about an hour into the service, he whispered over to me, and told me that he was leaving, and would be waiting for me in the car, once I got out of service, and he would take my grandson along with him.

Since keeping track of time wasn't something I did once I got caught up in the sermon, music and service itself, I hadn't realized that it was about 1:30 pm. Then he came to tap me on the shoulder from behind, sending my grandson to sit by me. He said in an un-whispered and angry tone, "I thought that you said, the service was over at 1 pm." I replied, and said "Look, I can't help it, if it's going over."

He told me, I should've gotten up and left, and see how inconsiderate you are. Here take your car keys, he said, I am leaving. I had never felt so embarrassed in church, because people had started looking and staring. When I did get out of church around 2 pm, I expected him to be long gone, but he was sitting inside the car waiting. He told me, the reason he had not left was because, once he got back to the car, he realized he had forgotten to wind the windows up. By the way, this was dead in the summer time. He didn't want to leave the car like that, nor did he want to come back into the church to retrieve the keys.

    I was about to drive when he suggested that he would drive. Of course, I didn't think anything of it, and gave him the keys. Moments later within the drive, he brought it up again, how inconsiderate I was for not leaving out of service. I tried to explain that I wasn't and how was I to know, the service would run over. I don't pay attention to time when I get to church. He then said, "See that's what I am talking about, let's see if you make it home today, because I am about to end it all right now." He then mashed down on the accelerator so hard, getting up to 60-65 miles per hour on city streets, dodging in and out cars, trucks, and riding on buses bumpers, missing from crashing by the skin of his teeth. I was yelling and screaming, begging him to slow this car down right now, and to have some consideration with my grandson in this car. At the same time, I was calling on the name of Jesus, to save us also, at which point, he finally slowed down to normal speed, and I could see how scared he even was, because his heart was beating so fast. He then said, "See the kind of things you make me do, when you make me angry." I had no more words left for him, because I was still shaken by the fact, we all could've just been killed.

His drama seemed so out of control, he was volatile. I feared for my safety and that of my grandson, because I knew what he was capable of.

There weren't always scary moments trying to tolerate "Kerry." We shared a few happy times occasionally, that lasted liked a couple of months, then he'll crack again.

During the good times, we'll do things like catch a movie, go out to breakfast or dinner, go clothes or household shopping and attend family gatherings together. A few times even, once I got off from work, and knew that he would be working until his part-time job closed at 11 pm, I'll ride the train to his job from work, and wait until he got off. While waiting, I'd watch how he provided excellent customer service and showed so much politeness to all his co-workers.

I asked him once doing the good times, how was it that he treated his co-workers and customers so nice, and me like crap. His response was because "I get paid."

As we all know, there are two sides to every story and I'll be the 1st to admit, I am far from perfect. I have some flaws also. Occasionally, we were able to have a decent dialogue to find out what he did and what I did. This was a sign of maturity.

I somehow just kept convincing myself that I'm going to make this relationship work. I've made everything work before. Sometimes the words he said, seemed like razor blades cutting me into ribbons. He would have a look on his face that was very censorious (critical). He had a way of intimidating you. He would go nuts over the least little things. Like another time for instance, anyone that knows me, can tell you that I love buying small souvenirs. So on one of my shopping sprees, I'd bought me a grey Mary Virgin statue, and brought it home and placed it on the wall unit. The next day, I looked for it, and it was gone. I looked everywhere in the house for it, and then saw it, thrown into the trash can.

I knew my daughter Tameka would never do nothing like this, so I asked him, did he. It was like, he despised every time I asked him "did he," or "why did you." He was easily riled, but he flicked off, raising his voice very high, until it was always scary, yelling like a coo-coo bird. He was, saying I'm getting sick and tired of you keep buying all of these little nick knacks around the house, crowding it up. I said to him at that point, do you realize that was a religious statue, and he responded, I don't care what the "F," it was, it was crowding up space.

He'd made me so mad at that point, after saying that, the next thing that came out of my mouth was, do you realize that this is my house, and I can buy whatever I want for it. "Yes," I do, he said yelling at the top of his lungs, and I don't give an "S," I'm moving the "F" out of here, soon as I find me a place. I said well, good then, let me know if you need some help looking. "Oh, so you trying to be funny "B," I'll break your "Mother F" neck. I then walked away, because I could tell he was about to explode into another one of his rages. Then he pulled me by the ear demanding that I listen to him.

I'd become accustom to his behavior, and just took what he ditched out to me, most of the time. I thought that he'd been hurt enough and I guess in his own way, he was seeking retribution. I wanted to believe that he'd really changed, but "boy" was I wrong.

He was always affable and pleasant around family and friends, but behind closed doors, the man was a dead man walking.

I'd avoided telling the police, because he'll threaten me with saying, you'll be dead by the time they get here, and I took that at face value. Along with the fact he was still on parole and I didn't want to live with that guilt on my shoulders again.

Another chilling moment that occurred with the coo-coo bird, was when one night I was watching my soap operas upstairs on the big T.V. (now anybody that knows me, will be able to tell you that I am a big soap opera fan). I would record them five days a week, and watch them at night after I got home from work, and finished all my household chores.

He comes up there, apparently bothered by that and turns the TV off, he unplugged all the connecting sockets, DVD, and cable box and says I dare you to put your hands on it. I demanded him to cut the TV back on right this minute, but he just ignored me and walked out. To say, I felt like a prisoner in my own home is an understatement.

I suffered more psychological and verbal than physical abuse from him. I didn't talk to many people about what went on behind closed doors in my household, because I've always been a very private person, not one to tell my business, like that, so I kept quiet and tried to deal with it on my own.

I realize now, that I'd went into the marriage with the wrong motives, under the assumption that I was responsible for what happened in the past, and now I was in a predicament to save him.

Whenever I'd tell him that I've had enough and was ending our relationship, he'd cry and beg me not to. I'm never going to hurt you again, he'd promise. So the cycle continued, explosions, promises, sweetness, and new explosions all over again.

Thinking back on my life with "Kerry," I can remember one thing after another going wrong. Sometimes, I felt like my life was being cursed with this man. Imagine that, all that apparent "bad luck," circumstances weren't just random coincident, they were the curses of God, because I'd married "Satan" himself. Like the Israelites, I'd not paid attention to all the red flags, until it was too late.

Psalm 145:14 - "The Lord upholds all that fall, and raises up all those that are bowed down." (KJV)

THE BIG FALL
Chapter 3

On December 31, 2008, my 43rd Birthday, I was on my way to New York City to splurge all day for my birthday. Kerry was to drop me off on his way to work, in front of the Martin Luther King Jr. library downtown. It was where my bus would depart.

The morning turned sour, because after learning from my daughter that "Kerry," had been acting childish. He was hanging up on her phone calls every time someone called, as if she didn't live there. So early that morning about 5:00 am, while he was driving, I thought it was a good time to ask him, "Why was he hanging up on "Tameka's," phone calls? His response shocked me, like a shock-wave, "I don't have to answer to why I've been doing that," I pay the "F" phone bill, and bla, bla, bla. We got into a heated argument, and by the time he got me to my drop off point, he had started speeding. He had not come to a full stop, before telling me to get the "F" out of his car. I said gladly, I opened the door and he didn't even wait for me to close it, he took off so fast, letting the cold brisk wind close the door for him. I had never felt so embarrassed, because people that were waiting for the bus saw what had just happened. I tried to smile it off. I walked around the corner to a McDonald's to get me some hot coffee and a breakfast sandwich. I was determined that I wasn't going to let him ruin the rest of my birthday, I had planned for months prior.

    When my bus arrived around 6:15 am, everyone got on, and went to a seat. I got me a window view, because I didn't want to miss anything. I relaxed back and enjoyed the 4-hour ride. Once there I took a tour bus to tour the city, on one of those double decker buses, and it was awesome. Then I had lunch and went to my scheduled performance to see the "Rocketts" at the Apollo Theatre, and it was so magical. After the show, I bought a few souvenirs, then I did a little shopping for my birthday, had dinner, then it was time for my bus to take me back to DC.

When I arrived back that night, it was late, close to midnight. I don't know why I was expecting Kerry to pick me up, after knowing how our morning had ended, but I was still hopeful. I arrived back about 11:00 pm, and no "Kerry" waiting for me, so I flagged down a cab to take me home. When I arrived home, he was there along with my daughter. I had bought her a couple of gifts back, so she was happy to receive them. I still thought about him, bringing him a bag of these glazed peanuts that were sold at a peanut stand. I know how he loves sweets, and those little nuts were so good, I bought back a few bags. I could tell that he was still mad at me, so I just placed them on his night stand.

OK now, it's about to be mid-night, the morning of "New Year's" day, and everyone was calling to wish us "Happy New Year's." I managed to put my madness to the side and wish him "Happy New Year's." He ignored me coldly. But one particular phone call, came from his "Dad," I answered the phone, so I thanked him for the Birthday card and money he had left for me, then wished him a "Happy New Years!!!" I then hollered for Kerry to pick up the phone. While he was on the phone, I could hear his side of the conversation, he was telling his Dad, that he was so mad at me, he felt like breaking my got damn neck. I immediately had a chill in my bones, because I received that as a threat. I don't know what his father told him back on the phone. I probably will never know that! But once again, I'd incriminated myself in the letter to Mr. Snyder, stating this also.

All I do know is, when I went to bed that night, I slept with one eye open and one closed. Luckily I did, because I awoke sometime in the middle of the night, to find him standing over me, looking weird and crazy. I asked him, what was he doing and what did he want? He said, get up, no one's sleeping tonight, and snatched the covers from off of me. "I said, look here, you better leave me alone, I ain't got time for this," and I'm tired now. But he kept insisting that I get up, and so the argument began (to tell you the truth, I can't even remember right now what the argument was about), but it got pretty heated, to the point, I was calling my "mom," in the wee hours of the morning. Whenever he started threatening me again, I'll call her to calm him down, somehow it seemed to work all the time. My hopes for us were high and my disappointments were bitter.

  For the next two weeks almost, we did our usual typical thing, going to bed silent and angry and waking up the next morning, the same way. We'll pass one another in the house, like two complete strangers unknown and nonexistent to each other. I wanted it to work so bad that I just kept ignoring all the signs. I stayed in self-denial.

Normally, I had to be the first one to break the ice, resulting in me needing something like, calling to his attention, a bill to be paid, needing something extra picked up from the grocery store, or a business phone call. But this particular time, I had to break the ice, with something a lot different. I so desperately needed a chauffeur to take me to and from "Georgetown" to the 1st Black President, "Obama's" Inauguration Ball. I didn't want to drive myself, because going up there, the traffic would have been too much. With all the Inauguration festivities, and the parking would have been too expensive, so I had to bargain with the devil.

I went to him, with this proposition, I said, "Kerry," I need a ride to the "Inauguration Ball," and once it's over, to come back and pick me up. He said, "what's in it for me," I said, well, I figured since we haven't had sex in a while, we could make love. He was like, oh yeah, let's do it then, and you got yourself a chauffeur. He dropped me off and picked me up on time. I had the most magical evening being at a black president's inauguration ball. All the ladies were decked out in lavish gowns or short-cut dresses like myself. I wore this gorgeous white and black spaghetti strap gown, with white laced panty-hose and some black pumps, along with my black-furred coat. You couldn't tell me nothing (LOL). "Kerry," always loved taking pictures of me, but then again, I believe he was camera-addicted to taking pictures of anything or anyone.

Ok, now things are all good with us again. We continue on with our normal husband and wife routine. Most times, "Kerry," would pick me up at the metro station, five minutes from the house, so I didn't have to walk home in the dark alone. I thought this was so sweet of him, because he would surprise me, in doing that. Sometimes he would have even prepared dinner, if he had time, since he arrived home before me, if he didn't have to work his part-time job that evening.

On January 26, 2009, I was summoned for jury duty. A little less than a week, from when I was just having a great week, doing something different every day involved around the Inauguration events. I did some sight-seeing, ate either lunch or dinner at a nice restaurant, and went to an event at the "Kennedy Center." I shopped for souvenirs for the President's Inauguration, "both downtown and around George Washington Hospital." I went to the President's speech at the "Lincoln Memorial" with a couple of friends and video-taped the event. Then the next day, I looked at the "President's" swearing in on T.V. at home. I made preparations and took the train downtown to wait for the parade to come down Pennsylvania Avenue.

It was freezing temperatures in the 30s that day, but I didn't care, because I was dressed warm and determined to see history in the making. I will never forget that day!

I arrived for "Jury Duty" on that Wednesday morning, I reported into the clerk, and went down the hall to the assigned room number where everyone sat, waiting for their juror number to be called. I was actually hoping that I would be called to serve, so that I could get a few days break from work. Lo and behold, my number was called. I went through the procedure and was actually selected to serve as a juror for a drug case. I was going to be Juror #9, and looking forward to my first time ever serving. The judge informed all of us jurors to report back on February 2nd at 9 am, as this would be the day the defendant's trial was to begin.

I went back to work on that Thursday morning. The following Friday, I was off, ran a couple of errands that morning, and afternoon, I drove down to "Waldorf, Maryland" to have my income taxes prepared. Lastly, I went to Sam's Club to do some shopping, while I was in the area.

By the time I got back home late that afternoon, I had only a few hours to get some sleep, before getting back up to go to my part-time "security officer" job. Normally, how it worked, as I was ready to leave out for work, "Kerry would be just getting in from his part-time job for the night.

Generally, once I got off in the mornings at 8 am, I would have to drive straight to my full-time job, but this was my weekend off, so I could go right home, bathe, get me a little nap, then get up and prepare myself an adventurous day. I remember going to pick up my grandson, and keeping him for the weekend, although I had to go back to work that "Saturday" night, my daughter would keep him over night until I got back home that "Sunday" morning.

We had a long day I ended it by spending hours in "Macy's." It had already turned dark, and I needed to get home to get some sleep for work that night. My grandson loves KFC, macaroni and cheese, so I drove over to the one inside the same shopping center as "Macy's," and got him his favorite, and me something as well.

Once I arrived home, I put my grandson to bed, because he was exhausted from me having him out all evening. I just had about two hours or less to sleep, get up take a shower, and head off to my part-time job.

When I awoke to start getting ready, I discovered that my youngest daughter, "Tameka," still hadn't come home. So I phoned her to see her where-abouts. She told me that her friend's mom was dropping everyone off, and she would be there a little late.

"Kerry," arrived shortly like he normally does, before I am about to leave. I was assuming that he would be in for the night, but once I informed him that I needed him to stay with "Keshawn," as he was still asleep, until "Tameka," arrived, that's when he told me that he was going back out for the night, and couldn't. I begged him practically, just until my daughter came home, then he could leave, he agreed finally, otherwise I would have never left my grandson home alone. So off to work, I went.

Once I arrived at work, relieved the officer before me, settled in, conducted my rounds, and then came back downstairs to my desk. I knew I needed to call back home to see if "Tameka," had got in yet, but there was no answer on the house phone, so I called her on her cell. This is when she told me that she wouldn't be coming home for the night, because her friend's mother didn't feel like coming over that side of town, and had dropped her off to my baby sister's house, along with her daughter instead.

I then tried to reach my husband "Kerry," to inform him of this, to let him know that I didn't want to interfere with his plans, and if he still needed to go, he could just drop my grandson off on his way, but there was no answer on the house phone, nor his cell. I just assumed that he perhaps had changed his mind, and went on to sleep, so I brushed it off, as just that being the case.

But, I couldn't have been more wrong. I received a call from my next door neighbor about 3 am that morning, informing me that she didn't want to alarm me, but she remembered, I had given her my number a while back in case of an emergency. The reason for her call, was to let me know that my grandson, had wandered from out of my house, setting off the burglary alarm, in the process, coming over to her house, in just his pajamas, no coat or shoes, just his socks and was shivering cold. Now remind you, it was about 20 degrees that cold and frigid night of February 1. She went on to say that she just happened to be up, because she had just gotten in and was wondering who could be coming to her house this time of night. She said when she looked through the peek-hole, she couldn't see anyone, but by us having the big bay window beside the door, she then peeked through the venetian blinds and saw this little boy that looked like my grandson. When she opened the door, she asked him, little man what are you doing outside this time of night, he was shivering and said, "they left me," and that's when she brought him inside.

She went on to say that the policeman were at my house, due to the burglary alarm going off, and that she would go over to let them know that she had the homeowner on the phone, and wouldn't let them know that my grandson was home alone. "I thanked her for that." She put the policeman on the phone, he asked who I was, then told me that he went through the house and found nothing out of place or unordinary that he could see, but would hang around for a little while longer. I thanked him and he then passed the phone back to Mrs. Holloway, my neighbor, she then assured me that my grandson was fine, and that I didn't need to leave work, and my grandson could stay there until I got off in the morning. I told her I couldn't believe he'd left him alone like this, and I appreciated her offer. I thought it best I came home to get him, because he isn't use to strangers, and eventually he would probably go into his crying tantrums. So, I really needed to get there, and she said OK, and we ended the conversation.

I gathered my things together and locked the building up. Since there was no traffic that time of night, I was home in about fifteen minutes. Once I turned onto my street "Tubman Road", I saw a policeman car sitting there, so I slowed down, as "I approached the stop sign" … Then proceeded around the block, into the alley of my driveway and parked. By the time I had gotten there, I could see "Kerry's" car parked in front of the house. Once I got out of my car and went into my house through the back door, he was coming through the front door with my grandson, not saying a word or anything. I proceeded upstairs, so I could get my grandson dressed and bring him back to work with me, until I got off from work later that morning.

Once I got my grandson's clothes and coat on, and was prepared to leave back out, it bothered me that "Kerry," still was not saying a word to me. By then he was in the bathroom, brushing his teeth, so I approached him, asking him, what kind of man are you without a "heart and soul" to leave a little boy in the house alone, this time of night.

He finishes brushing his teeth, then comes up to me fast, pointing his finger in my face, yelling and saying, "I knew it, I knew it," just knew you were going to blame me for this "shit." I said, well who else I am supposed to blame, I left you in the house with him. "No," he said, you should be blaming your "Bitch Ass" daughter. Then he surprisingly lifted me up, threw me onto our bed, slammed me down face down and continued jerking me up and down by my collar, yelling at me like a crazy man, gone mad. I was yelling out to him to "stop it," and to "get off of me." He yanked me up, still by the back of my collar, and then threw me up against the wall, still yelling like a mad man. At this point, my grandson is crying and scared. He tells me at some point, that he is going to take me out of my misery and to stay here. I say, I'm calling the police right now, he says, by the time they get here, you will be dead, "Bitch." I'm going to end this "shit" tonight! Then he ran down the stairs to the 1st level. The first thing I thought was, oh my God, I'm going to die!

Now I am in a panic, not knowing what he is going to do or thinking of for sure, so I run upstairs, my grandson in pursuit behind me. Once I reached the top landing, I go into my closet, where I knew I hid my "38" and loaded a bullet into the chamber. I then placed it into my waistband, hiding it with my long winter coat. I then paced the floor, hoping that he would perhaps just leave the house and go somewhere to cool off. But then I suddenly heard him coming back up the stairs fast, yelling again and cursing, as he got to the top of the landing. I could see the rage in his face. He then grabbed a pair of "6" inch green scissors that was in the desk caddy, he tempted to approach me, while pointing to my closet and screaming at me, asking "what color dress do you want to be buried in"? I was frozen and lost for words at that point, and something inside me just told me that this is it "Moe," it's either you or him. I feared for my life and that of my then 5-year old grandson that was standing beside me the entire time. I reached for the "38", as he was coming towards me, and I fired one shot, without knowing or realizing where I had hit him.

Instantly, he dropped the scissors and reached for the phone that was on the desk also, in an attempt to call 9-1-1, that's when he collapsed and blood started spurting from his mouth.

Still unaware of what I had just done, to say I was in shock of what I have just done, is an understatement, but I got my cell phone from out of my pocket and immediately called 9-1-1, and reported that I had just shot someone, my husband. The operator asked for my name and address, then asked me where he was shot at, and I told her, I didn't know, but to hurry and hung up the phone. I then called my daughter to tell her what I had just done and to hurry and get here to get "her son," before the police arrived. Then I called my sister

"Jackie," to tell her the same thing, and then my mom. I went over to Kerry to see if he was still breathing, he was faintly, and I said to him, I was sorry, but he made me do it, and to hang on, help is on the way.

I then started picking up things out of place upstairs. I ran down stairs to hide the gun under my bedroom pillow. I started straightening up things in there, as if I was getting ready for guess. All the time, not realizing that I was covering up evidence.

I finally realized it was a lot of banging downstairs at the front door, and ran down to open it, to see the police officers. I told them on the spot, that my husband is upstairs and "he tried to kill me," and "I shot him."

The female officer took me over to my sofa, sat me down and started questioning me, asking me did I have any marks on me, did I need to go to the hospital and things like that. Then the male officer yelled down to ask me, where was the gun, and I told him. The paramedics arrived, and it wasn't long before they were bringing him down on the stretcher, his shirt was off and he had an oxygen mask on him. The officer allowed me to call my supervisor to inform him of this emergency and that I wouldn't be coming back to work. I needed him to go to the post and wait for my sister to bring him the keys.

    I hope these first three chapters has given you a little more insight, as to what I was thinking on that fatal night, because I felt really nervous writing it.

Psalms 46:1 – God is our refuge and strength, a very present help in trouble (If God brings you to it. He will bring you through it)

CHAPTER 4
THE ARREST AND BOOKING

Shortly afterwards, I was being patted down, put under arrest and being read my amendment rights. The officer took the keys from me and gave them to my sister.

As I was being lead outside, I could see my sister, my baby brother, my daughter and her friend. I just cried out to them, telling them how sorry I was, as I was being placed in the back of a police cruiser, for what I had just done. It felt like a nightmare on Elm Street. Tears were just streaming down my face.

We arrived at the "Police" headquarters, it seemed like no time. They took me into the interrogation room, where I would give my statement, or I could waive my rights, until I was in the presence of an Attorney. I choose to waive my rights and talk then, because I felt like I had nothing to hide and the truth was the truth, as to what happened earlier.

    I learned months later from my attorney that I was being secretly recorded in that little room. He showed me the video of me sitting there and practically passed out, when I was left alone, for what seemed like hours. At that point, while there, that's when I learned from the homicide detective that "Kerry," had expired. I nearly passed out with the deliverance of the news. He told me that he had expired at 5:55 am, so it was about 2 hours later from the time it had happened.

    As daybreak was approaching, they brought me a breakfast sandwich from McDonald's. (I didn't think this would be my last real outside food, from the real world), but it was. Before leaving they allowed my daughter to bring me another coat, my eye-glasses, and take back some things I wasn't allowed to have, but I couldn't see or talk to her then.

Next, I was taken down to central –cell block, where I was booked, finger-printed, and allowed to make one phone call. After being processed in, they took me into another room that had cold-metal bunk-beds with no mattress. It was freezing cold in there, so my coat came in handy for a blanket.

After being there for what seemed liked hours, I and others, were all loaded into the patty-wagon, and taken down to the D.C. Jail. Sad to say, I use to work there ten years prior, never in a million years, thought that one day, I would be an inmate on the other end. Once there, I was processed in after several hours and taken upstairs to where I would be housed.

The next morning of February 2nd 2009, I was awakened and taken downstairs to await for the Marshalls to take me and others to court, it would be my first court appearance.

Remember, when I told you earlier in the book, that I was selected for jury duty, well instead the same day of appearing to serve as a juror, I was appearing as a defendant my own self, now picture that!

Once at the DC Superior Court, I was given a cup to pee in, for a drug test, and my sweater vest was taken off of me, which I learned later was to be tested for fingerprints, and then I waited to be assigned an Attorney. I didn't learn until years later, that I was assigned the best public defender attorney for my defense, but I don't fault my sisters, because they didn't know, needing an Attorney to my degree, was a first for all of us.

They came across a private investigator that was soliciting his supervisor's services, as a fake want to-be Johnny Cochran extension to the original man himself, and not knowing any difference, they bought into it and hired this man to represent me.

He came to the area, where all attorneys would meet and talk to their clients for the first time.

He introduced himself to me as Mr. McCants, my new Attorney that my family had retained, and that he would be representing me. He then asked me for details of what happened. Confessing what I had done was a load lifted off of my shoulders.

1 John 1:9 tells us, if we confess our sins he is faithful and just and will forgive us our sins and purify us from all unrighteousness

He listened attentively, then told me I would be coming out soon for my arraignment. Shortly thereafter, I was led by two Marshalls shackled into the courtroom of Judge Michael Rankins. I entered that courtroom looking like I had been hit by a freight train. I was still dressed in part of my part-time security job uniform, the grey pants and white shirt. Remember, I told you earlier that they had taken the vest from me, my hair was a complete mess, and there I was in a court room full of people, and it was packed, between all of his family and all mines, and other speculators, that I couldn't tell you, who was who. It was so packed that some had to stand up. I spotted my sisters and mom right away.

I had never felt so embarrassed in my entire life. Never in a million, could I ever imagine myself being led shackled into a courtroom, for what I was being charged for, second-degree murder while armed.

The judge asked me how did I plea, guilty or not guilty. I said not guilty, after that my attorney did the rest of the talking for me. He had asked for a bond for me, but the judge denied it, and I was returned back to the custody of the DC Jail.

After a long two weeks at the county, what seemed like forever, I was scheduled and returned for my next court appearance on February 17, 2009, another preliminary hearing. Once again, no bond was granted.

I was so looking forward to going home, but I would be spending the next couple of months, back at the county until my next court appearance, which was scheduled for April 17, 2009, and again back on May 1, 2009.

In between these dates, I had a shred of hope, that once blood splattered results came back, and my story was believed, they would drop the charges.

But, on August 26, 2009, I received the next shock of my life, after calling home and receiving this news from my sister, she told me that the grand jury had indicted me, because they learned I also stabbed him. The autopsy showed he had punctured wounds on his neck and arms. I nearly passed out, right there where I was standing, because I was receiving the most unbelievable story that they could come up with, just to find some kind of justification to hold me. I just cried out to my sister, "no, no," that's not true, I didn't do that to him. Somebody's trying to frame me now. The Officer's had colluded in a fabrication to better justify the arrest.

Sometime within that week my attorney visited me and re-informed me of the indictment and my next court appearance, would be in a couple of days, August 28, 2009.

I appeared this time, and again granted no bond. I would be returning back to the county jail, until my next status hearing, January 2010. Those seemed to be the longest waiting months of my life, waiting in limbo, as your fait is to be decided.

In between that time, my attorney visited me and his private investigator on a few occasions, to keep going over my defense.

Exodus 14:14 – "The Lord himself will fight for you. Just stay calm!"

CHAPTER 5
ADAPTING TO JAIL

I am extremely blessed to be able to say I never became addicted to drugs or alcohol. I just straight-out did not like either. I tried it once in my early adult-hood and it just didn't agree with me. So I was in my semi-right frame of mind that fatal night. I always had a lot of self- control. It was part of my personality not to let anything control me, but that night was different. I acted on impulse, from all the past and current threats embedded in my memory, and emotions, and perhaps I felt the effects of it, repeating itself and acted them out according to his words.

While going through the process, I felt bitter about having my very good reputation taken away. It was one of my good qualities, I didn't want to lose, my reputation. I know, I probably don't have much of one now, because once you become a murderer, there are certain groups of people where I will never be one of the girls' again. I get it though, "murder is a sin," but it hasn't stopped the Kingdom of God, from still accepting me.

From the time I was arrested on February 1, 2009, to the time, I was sentenced on March 2010, and June 2010, being released from the county and into the custody of federal prison, which averages out to about sixteen months, it was extremely hard for me, because I had never been away from my family this long period of time.

I talked to them on the phone more frequently because all the calls were local, and they visited me every other week. In between the week they didn't come, a co-worker/friend visited me regularly. He was just a friend that was concerned about me, but his visits meant a lot to me.

The visits there consisted of 1-hour contact visits and only forty-five minutes on holidays. I loved getting visits, but despised how they ended. It's hard watching your love-one's leave out and you can't go with them. The next difficult part, was after the visit, everyone had to be strip-searched, butter-ball naked all together. We were all lined up behind a table, and asked to take off one item at a time, to be placed on the table, then once everything was off, we were instructed to turn around squat and cough. I had never felt so humiliating in all my entire life. But after every visit, this would be required, to ensure no contraband was being smuggled into the facility.

    Everywhere you needed to go throughout the county, leaving from your unit, you had to be escorted by an officer, either by the elevator or stairs, to your visits, religious church services, health services, rec and the holding cell in preparation for court.

    Outside of these places, you were being confined to your unit all day, which consisted of an average size day room, a small TV room, an open multi-purpose room, four tiers of cells, with one shower on each floor, depending on what unit you were on. Some of the toilets were in the room and some were outside the cells, which allowed you to open the doors from the inside.

I was fortunate for the last year of my stay there, because I had a single room cell to myself.

It was great because you never know who you could end up with as a cell mate, some women may be just coming off the streets from detoxing, looked like men, homeless, or rough rats. There were a few mature women like myself that came through as well. But, every night before getting into that bed, I'd get down on my knees on that cold concrete floor, to say my prayers.

During my stay here, is where I really got to know "God," like I never knew him before. Who would've thought I'd get to know him the way I did, but I really got to know him in a better way for myself.

Now folks don't get me wrong here, let me clarify myself, I've been a born-again Christian, since I was a teenager, up until my arrest. I went to church regularly, had been a member, within the past two decades to "The United House of Prayer for all People," Union Temple" and "The Believer's Worship Center," which is where I was last present.

I had been baptized several times over a period of my life time and while at this county jail. I was re-baptized again in April 2009, I had to get this sin off of me, and as it says in 2 Corinthians 5:7, I was a new creation in Christ. I also needed God to create in me a clean heart, and put a new and right spirit within me (Psalm 51:10), because Christ can forgive any sin. And his spirit is at work even within prison walls.

"God," knew that I had to be strong enough to handle the trials and tribulations, I would be facing.

I set a goal for myself to read the entire Bible within three months. I started from Genesis, reading ten chapters a day, until I reached Revelation. In fact, I read it twice, along with taking a one year Bible course through Crossroads.

I was blessed during my time at the CCA. Every day during mail call, my name would be called several times, because letters, cards and money came from so many different people. To tell you the truth, I almost felt like a celebrity at times, who had to answer to all my fan mail. By the time I was sentenced, I had accumulated about two tall trash bags, of all those letters and cards. I hated, I had to discard them all, because I wasn't allowed to take anything to the feds with me. The ladies would say to me, girl you sure do have a lot of people that love you.

Most of the letters, were about family or friends, being concerned, wanting to know what had happened, offering their condolences or sharing the same common adversity of having been there before also.

I received a couple of magazine subscriptions and the Washington Post newspapers, during my tenure as well, to past some of time away, and shared them after I finished reading with any of the other ladies, who wanted to read them. Then my sister and best friend, I grew up with would both download me books from off the computer and send them to the jail for me. My time in that jail had served a great purpose. I've seen a lot of faces come and go. I've learned a lot about myself and others. I've learned the meaning behind "just sitting still…" I learned by the end of the year, while here that DC homicides for 2009 was 143, "14" at the time of his.

    Periodically, I would have my Attorney visits and sometimes he would send his private investigator over, to come and talk with me, to get me off the unit for a while, when he couldn't make it.

    Visits from my Attorney started off frequently, then as my court dates started, there were large gaps until the next court appearance, so the visits lessen.

Well during one of those large gaps, I did the unthinkable, and it turned out to be the most stupid mistake, I could have ever made in my entire life.

Being that I had never been in trouble before to this extent, I thought that the prosecutor was someone I could trust, open up to, and that was pretty much on my side also, as my attorney. I later find out I couldn't have been more wrong.

I wrote the prosecutor a seven-page letter, explaining to him, all the different encounters, me and "Kerry" had, when he exploded and the family members of his that were there to witness it, and he could verify it from them. It was a very detailed letter. After writing it, I told my sister about it, and she did ask me, are you sure you want to do this, because you never write the other side who is trying to prosecute you. I said, I'm sure, I think, it'll be okay, without informing my Attorney. So off the letter went. I mailed it directly to the prosecutor's office. I wonder why weeks, then months went by and I still hadn't received a direct response back from this man.

Finally, I went back to court on another status hearing, and while I was inside the cell, behind the judge's chambers, my Attorney came back to talk to me each time, to let me know what to expect, once I came inside. Well, this time, he wasn't too happy. The prosecutor handed him a copy of the letter I had written to him. This is when I learned, that I had done the stupidest thing in my life. I had provided incriminating statements to them. He ridiculed me, and told me that letter may mess me up big time and I should have sent it to him first, to review. I was like, oh no, I didn't know it would hurt me, I thought he would understand some of the things I went through. He said from now on, if I am to represent you, please do not write any more letters to the prosecutor. I told him, I wouldn't.

Another one of the hardest times for me, was the longer I remained at "CCA" was that every time I looked out my cell room's window, you could see so much of home, the fact that you were so close and couldn't get there, was mental torture. I could see "Marbury Plaza" from a hall window, I use to look out all the time, and from my window, I could see the cemetery and the basketball court.

Being close to home also allowed me to still be able to listen to familiar radio stations that I loved listening to, like "Steve Harvey's" morning show in the morning, and in the afternoon "Michael Basiden" and Coco brother, which I'd listen to until I fell asleep. My favorite song, that I had to wait for before I could fall asleep, because I knew it was going to be played, was "It ain't over," by Maurette-Brown Clark."

Because, somehow in my spirit, I knew that no matter what was going to happen, after I had taken a plea or went to trial, I was going to be okay. "God," doesn't give us any more than we can bear, and I believed that he would never leave me nor forsake me.

It was very comforting to know that so many people on the outside were praying for me. I prayed fervently day and night myself.

I was blessed that a month-an-a-half after my arrest, my baby sister GG had only been renting a condo through her in-laws, therefore making it easy for her to break free and move into my recently brand new townhome, otherwise I would have lost it to foreclosure.

The astonishing part about this, is I hadn't asked my sister to do this, it was the farthest thing from my mind, but "God" touched her heart, spoke to her spirit, and told her, this was what she needed to do, to be a blessing to her older sister.

At the time, my youngest daughter was sixteen years old and eleven months, so she would also act as her guardian, until she reached eighteen, and could then be responsible for herself. So my attorney had the guardianship papers drawn up for me to sign. Luckily, also my daughter had one more year left before finishing and graduating from High School.

Another great miracle that turned out, to benefit both my sisters, was GG didn't have to sell any of her furniture or put them into storage, because my other sister, "Jackie" hadn't had any furniture yet, so she moved her furniture in her house, and it ended up being a win-win situation for them both, as GG's furniture was practically new also, as mine.

Nine months after I had been there, my younger brother "Tyrone," was on his way home from prison, after serving five years. I hadn't seen him in about a couple of years, and couldn't wait to see him, just not in this predicament. But he hadn't been home quite two weeks, before having time to settle down and obtain his driver's license and he was up there to visit me.

I'm telling you, it was like a Kodak moment, when we reached one another in that visiting room. Now mind you, our family is a bunch of crybabies we both hugged one another so hard, and we both cried at the same time. My sister "Jacqueline," finally had to say, you two stop it, before you make me cry.

It pained my brother to see his oldest sister in this predicament, to be facing what I had on my back. Now imagine that he was just coming home, and I was on my way to prison for what would probably be a very long time.

"God," always lines up things the way they are supposed to be, in Isaiah Chapter 55, where God said "for as the heavens are higher than the earth, so are my ways higher than your ways, and my thoughts than your thoughts (v.9).

I am now down to one month left before my trial is set to begin, when I receive a visit from the pre-sentencing probation office services. I am escorted from CCA over to the DC Jail to where this would take place.

It was done by video camera, and I would be asked a series of questions about my childhood and up- bringing, my education, work history and criminal history. As I talked, he wrote down everything I said. He told me this is the report, that the judge would use when sentencing me, and that he was recommending me seventeen years, and I asked this man, how much time this charge carried if I was to be convicted of it. When he told me 40 years to life, I nearly fell out of that chair, and said to him, are you kidding me, he said "No ma'am" I'm not, do you have any more questions? I said "No Sir," I don't, then he said, well that concludes our interview.

I had to wait a while until an escort came back for me, and take me back to my unit. When I arrived back, I went into my room and dropped to my knees, praying to the father, please "Lord," please don't let that judge sentence me to forty years to life, in the name of Jesus!!

One week now before my trial, and I learned that the prosecutor, had my oldest daughter "Ekia," picked up and arrested to remain in custody at CCA, as well. This man was going to use my own daughter to testify against me, as to some incriminating information that she told him on the grand jury witness stand. I was never told this until the day my trial was to begin.

I had happened to call home and that's when my sister told me, what was going on and that she was being held here until my trial began.

It just so happened also, being that all the officers know me practically, informed me that my daughter was upstairs on E4-B, and that she had been crying and so scared. My heart ached for her, because I had no idea, what was going on.

Come the morning of my trial, everyone is awakened at 3:30 am in the morning to prepare for court. We are escorted downstairs to the holding area, fed breakfast, and then wait for the next couple of hours, to be picked up by the US Marshalls. Once they finally arrived, they'll call everyone out one by one, by name, and then chain us up, like the chain gang, along-side the wall.

I suddenly heard a tap on the window, behind me, and turned around to see that it was my daughter, "Kia." I didn't know that the correctional officers had orders to keep us separated and not to talk to one another. I got the attention of one officer, and told her that was my daughter in there, and could we go out together to the bus. She responded, and said, oh you're her mother, "no ma'am" you two are to have no contact. I said, how come, and she responded that, those are the orders given to us. So I just whispered, I love you, to her, and she told me to move away from the door.

Once me and all the other ladies were led unto the bus, and seated, they then locked the cage door up, but there are two seats opposite one another, in a small caged area alone. Next thing I saw the Marshalls were bringing, "Kia," on the bus to sit, in one of those seats. If I had known that, I would have sat closer to the front, but I was only like five rows away, and someone else had already sat in the first couple of rows. So we were only able to whisper back and forth to one another.

When we arrived at the Courthouse, they took "Kia," off the bus first, and into the building, while the rest of us had to wait.

Once it was our turn to be loaded off the bus, and into the courthouse, the standard procedure was they would split everyone up into two or three different cells, where we would sit for hours, until our names were called, to be escorted upstairs to the court room.

All of a sudden, in-between waiting, I saw the cell door opening, and "Kia," coming inside. I couldn't believe they were putting us together. We were able to hug, kiss and talk finally, and she was left in there for about half-an-hour, before someone realized they had made a mistake, by putting her in there with me. I didn't know it at the time, but this would be the *first of God's favor, watching over me.

I learned later on that morning from my Attorney, why "Kia" was there, and because of someone's slip up, in putting us together in the same cell, she was strike from being able to testify against me.

Psalm 56:3 - "Whenever I am afraid, I will trust in God"

CHAPTER VI
THE TRIAL

After waiting in limbo for a year and one month, the scary moment that I'd been waiting for had finally arrived, my trial began on March 9, 2010 and lasted for about 2 weeks, up until March 21, 2010.

I'd never felt more shy, nervous and embarrassed in my entire life. I've always had natural feelings of shyness, but my family and friends knew the content of my character. I knew that all eyes would be mainly on me, and the courtroom was very packed with all my family, friends, and supporters on one side, and "Kerry's" family on the other side.

A peace of calm had filled my spirit, because the night before, the "Holy Spirit" had spoken to me from Revelations 2:10, saying "Mozella," my child, "Do not fear any of those things which you are about to suffer. Indeed, the devil is about to throw some of you into prison, that you may be tested, but be faithful until death and I will give you the crown of life." (v.10)

The Lord understood, what I was about to go through, and what I would also face in the future. Our faith may be tested, so that we may trust his faithfulness. Fear is powerful; it can override logical thinking and produce irrational behavior.

During the entire time, I was on trial, I was able to wear a different suit each day that my sisters had picked out and put together for me. Although I still had to be shackled at the hand and feet, behind the defense table each day. The jurors couldn't see it, only the audience, as I would enter and depart from the courtroom each time.

Once the trial got started, which lasted for about 2 weeks, between testimonies and showing photographs. The jury heard the gruesome details.

Photos of the body were introduced and passed through the jury box. All this was to take away my self-defense claim, because the crime scene investigators didn't take the scissors into evidence for finger printing, so I could easily see how they ruled out self-defense. But I would've never done something that heinous to him and having to have to look at those pictures, gave me goose bumps, and leaving me to tremble under the table.

At trial also, the prosecutor brought up and displayed to the jurors, a list of positives and negatives I'd written down for "Kerry" to work on. Their purpose was to show a motive for the murder, again. I didn't write those things down, because I was planning to kill him one day. I'd written them down because I always thought it was cathartic to write things down, pretty much like when one keeps a diary or a journal.

Then a forensic expert testified that based on the blood-splatter results on the wall, I couldn't have been standing where I said I was (how could I've been exact, when it happened over a year ago). When a forensic expert says something appears to be or is consistent with the findings, that doesn't mean it is the only explanation. It just means it is one possible explanation, and one that fits the current forensic data.

I wanted to say a lot of things that would've connected all the dots, to their theory, but decided against it. You'll see what those things were in Chapter 7. I was afraid they'll hit me with obstruction of justice, added on to what I was already facing.

After my testimony, that concluded my trial, followed by the closing arguments from both sides. Then the Judge ran through the charges and the juror instructions. The jurors were to consider very briskly, despite their complexity.

The jurors could've found me guilty on the 2nd degree or of a lesser charge, manslaughter. The primary distinction between these was the issue of "intent." In order to find someone guilty of murder in 2nd degree, it must be shown that the accused both "intended" to kill and did so. To find someone guilty of manslaughter, by contrast, it need only be shown that the defendant acted "recklessly" and in doing so caused death.

Then they were all excused to start their deliberations. After their departure, I was then lead back into the cell-block behind the Judges' chambers, to await their verdict and my fate.

After only four hours had passed, the verdict was in and the Marshalls returned me back inside the courtroom. The Forman read each verdict of the five charges, which were all guilty. I knew I would be found guilty on the gun charges, because my firearm wasn't registered in the District of Columbia, only the state of Maryland, but still I was stunned and mortified. I felt like I'd humiliated everyone who believed in me.

It felt like to me, I was given no "justification," for my actions. Had anyone even considered that I reasonably believed my life and grandson was in imminent danger of such an assault and the actions I took led to his death, could certainly be justified and therefore, the jurors could've found me not guilty. But, never in a million years, did I think I would be found guilty of second-degree murder/while armed. "Hello," was anyone out there hearing me. It was self-defense! Obviously not, right? All I could do was just hang my head, as in disbelief. I couldn't even cry, as much as I wanted to scream out, because I knew that my family and friends were all watching me. I'd warned them all days before, that no matter what the verdict, I needed them all to remain calm and strong for me, even still….

More than ever, I was just glad that this ordeal had finally ended, guilty or not guilty. I needed for this ordeal to be behind me, so that I could move on with my own healing.

There I was a mild-mannered and shy person, one with no history of a violent crime before, but guilty of a grotesquely and cruel murder, according to the government and jurors.

The Judge then scheduled my sentencing about a month-and-half later, in May of 2010. It was a day, I dreaded, because I didn't know what that Judge was going to hit me with, after that probation officer had told me, I could get forty-to-life, but I prayed fervently that "God" wouldn't let him sentence me to anything close to that.

On the day of sentencing, the courtroom was packed with both families, on opposite sides. The Judge started by listening to my Attorney, then the prosecutor cited case laws, as to how much time I should be sentenced. Then he allowed all of my character witnesses to speak on my behalf, which consisted of my mother, my sister "Jacqueline," and our long-time family friend name "Kevin." Kerry's character witnesses consisted of his mother and a cousin. Lastly, it was my turn, in which I'd written a long apology letter to his family that I read aloud nearly choking on my tears.

The Judge gave his speech, then came my sentencing. For each conviction, he listed the amount of months separately, and then ran them all together to run concurrent, which consisted of 240 months. I wanted to pass out on the onset of hearing that, but since "God's" grace was sufficient for me in our weakness, he blessed me to stand strong.

Once I was sentenced, it felt like a ton of weight lifted off of my shoulders, in spite of me still trying to vision how in the world, I was going to do all of that time.

Philippians 4:13 – "I can do all things through Christ who strengthens me"

CHAPTER 7
THE GOVERNMENT'S JUSTIFICATION AND THEORY

I define me, not the government. Don't ever allow anyone to be your definition. Only choose someone who can add definition to your life.

They couldn't stop stressing enough, in every court arraignment, trial and motions drawn up, on how I didn't assist him with first aid, how none of the furnishing wasn't out of place, nor the bed, where I said he had thrown me unto. I couldn't explain it, at the time myself, maybe because my thought pattern was still in a ball of confusion, and I'd temporarily drifted out of reality, causing my "OCD" to kick in, a proverbs 31 woman characteristic.

You see, I assumed that once I made the initial first step of calling the 9-1-1 dispatcher, I'd done what I was supposed to, because I knew that I wasn't a doctor or a nurse and whatever condition he was in, was left up to "God." I should have received credit for not abandoning the scene, returning the next morning, in shock, hysterical and making it appear as if someone else had done it. I told him that I was so sorry and that help was on the way.

"Yes," I did start phoning my mom, sister and daughter secondly, then thirdly my "OCD" kicked in like I said before. Believe me when I tell you this: My mother instilled in me, since I was a teenager, to always make your bed before leaving the house, because you never know who may stop by unexpected. Your household is a reflection of you and should always be in order. That rule of discipline never left me, but resonated with me for many years to come, from the time I first left home at eighteen years old, until that fatal night. Any ex-boyfriend, sibling, guests, family and now I can add on any fellow inmates that have bunked with me during my years of incarceration, can tell you with certainty that "Mozella's" bed has to always be made.

It irks me to see a messy bed. My daughters can even confirm to what I am telling you that throughout the years of their up-bringing, whenever they were running late for school or perhaps didn't even make it up on purpose, when they returned home, their beds would be made. It was in my "DNA." This is what my spirit was exercised, disciplined and trained to do.

A proverbs 31 woman makes sure that nothing will be needed for her household or out of order. The proverbs 31 woman conditions her house to never run out. She's never caught off guard. She is a prepared woman, and whatever it takes, she is determined to be organized.

Next, the neighbors had told them and testified that I'd swirled into the driveway real fast and slammed the car door hard, after I've gotten out of it. From this statement, they went with their theory that I was in a rage, because of the fact he had left my then 5-year old grandson home alone.

Then a police officer testified that I had no scars on me, the bed was nicely made up and nothing on the upstairs level seemed out of place and he hadn't observed any scissors near the body.

Then a large photo was shown to the jurors with the scissors inside the caddy. All of this information was to take away my self-defense claim and you know the old adage saying "a picture alone is worth a thousand words."

I don't know why they were expecting to see any scars on me, when I clearly told them on more than one occasion, what he did, after I asked him that question. He rushed over to me yelling and pointing his finger in my face, then picked me up, and slammed me down unto the bed face down, jerking me up and down by the back collar of my vest, still ranting and raving, then pulled me up off the bed, then up against the wall, between the "armor dresser" and the window, jerking my head back and forth up against the wall, like a mad man in heat, while I stood there begging for him to stop hurting me, in front of my grandson.

"My Facts of their version"

Now we've all heard the saying also, that a dead man can't talk, so therefore all you have to rely on is what the living witness version is, and since that would be me, I am going to continue to share with you, the whole truth and nothing but the truth. The truthful lips shall be established forever, but the lying tongue, but for a moment (Proverbs 12:19). I would place my right hand on a bible, if you asked me to. Never, the less, James 5:12 tells us, do not swear either by heavens or by earth or with any other oath. But let your "yes" be "yes" and your "no," no, lest you fall into judgement. But, anyway these are the facts: Was I angry, "yes, I was," and who wouldn't have been, after learning that your 5 year old grandson was left alone and left out of the house in the middle of the 20 degrees night, with no clothes on; but angry enough to take his life for that "No," it went much deeper than that, when I saw him in action, threatening my life, by yelling and pointing, "what color dress did I want to be buried in?" Then moving towards me with the scissors in his hands. These words will forever be embedded into my memory. For the Word of God, says in Proverbs 18:21, "Death and life are in the power of the tongue; those words alone resonated so quickly, and I felt at that point, this means, its either you or me, and acting in fear of my life, I pulled my .38 from my waistband, not knowing where I was aiming and just fired one time. Not realizing in a million years, that one shot, would become fatal and ending his life.

    Afterwards, he dropped the scissors and reached for the phone, in an attempt to dial 9-1-1, and then he collapsed and fell. I then pulled out my cellphone and made the call to 9-1-1. After doing that, I called my "mom, my sister and then my daughter, to hurry and get here also, to pick up her son.

    Then it was like momentarily I lost awareness and started straightening the area up, picking up the ironing board that was knocked down, making sure the cushions on the sofa were in order, and I believe I may have also picked up the scissors from the floor and placed them back into the caddy, in which they belonged.

Next, I ran downstairs, placed my .38 revolver under one of the bed pillows, then I started straightening the bed up to look in place again, as though I was expecting guess and not the police officers. Still not realizing at the time, by doing all this, I was taking away my self-defense claim and making it look as though, I was fabricating my entire story. When in actual reality this is really what happen and what I had done afterwards.

When all these findings were brought out at trial, I wanted so bad to blurt out, the reason why everything was so neat in the house, but was too afraid, they would then hit me with "obstruction of justice." So all I could do was let it ride and pray for a miracle later to rescue me from out of the miry clay (pit).

Everyone that ever truly knew me, would be able to tell you that "Mozella," never leaves her house in a mess, beds have to be made, floor cleaned off, everything picked up, no dirty dishes in the sink, just in case unexpected guess ever stopped by.

I feared that he would over power me again, like downstairs in the bedroom, so I quickly drew the gun and fired. I thought to myself, "oh my God," this is it finally, this man could have dismembered me, so my enormous fear of him caused me to shoot without thinking of the consequences. The threat was vivid in my memory and believable, "what color dress do you want to be buried in?"

Then lastly, they did a good job on framing me, as if what I had done already wasn't enough. They made it look like I'd tried to cut or puncture him with some sort of sharp object, on his neck and forearms. When clearly, I've told them, I never touched him that night.

I believe what happened is one of these three things, although I will never be able to prove it, because the trial Attorney I had didn't investigate further into this as well, so I was defeated. (1) It could've happened in route to the hospital, while the paramedics tried to save his life; (2) It could've happened once in the emergency room, while being hooked up to all those different IVs, cutting him open, in attempt to remove the bullet to save his life; (3) I learned in the months before my trial, that a witness, was willing to testify to the fact that "Kerry" had showed up to her "Birthday" party with another woman. My theory to that, was maybe, since he did have alcohol in his system, he tried to fondle all over her, and in an attempt to fight him off, she scratched him up, in those places. You see, "Kerry," was a red-bone, so the least little thing of these three scenarios could bruise him up easily.

They took a fingernail analysis of my nails, right before my 1st court arraignment, and it came back negative. It was never proven in court, what would be the cause of those marks, only that the one gunshot to the chest is what killed him.

    Fourth theory is that while the police officer that ran upstairs to observe the situation, and described him being in a fetal position, telling him to hang on help was on the way, he could've easily used those scissors himself, to put those puncture or cut wounds there himself, then placed the scissors into the caddy, to take away my self-defense claim, that they heard me say, upon entering my house, so that they could insure their conviction.

    Sadly, no one will ever know the truth behind this, but me and "God" know that I didn't do it. The Lord Jesus knows how they framed me well on this and lied on me to make themselves look good, because we all know that there are so many crooks and devils right on the police force everywhere, but its ok, because the Lord God said in his Word, "Vengeance is mine." I'll admit though, there were times I was clearly mad, I was mad at God for setting up things the way he did. But, according to

Hebrews 12:6-7, for whom the Lord love he chasten and scourgeth every son whom he receiveth (v.7). If ye endureth chastening, God dealeth with you as with sons; for what son is he whom the father chastenth not?

But, I want to make a bold statement, right now. You see, I didn't kill "Kerry" that fatal night; his very own words did…. The Bible says in Proverbs 18:21 again, I'll reiterate it, "Death and life are in the power of the tongue, careful study of this scripture, tells us plainly that our words have consequences. Then Proverbs 21:23 puts it another way; he who guards his mouth and his tongue keeps himself from trouble. Matthew 12:34, what is in your heart comes out of your mouth, and lastly, Proverbs 16:9, tells us that a man's mind plans his way.

The Bible says that there is an appropriate time to speak (Ecclesiastes 3:7). Knowing the right time to speak is beneficial for both the speaker and hearer, whether they are words of love, encouragement or rebuke. Keeping silent also has its place and time.

Deuteronomy 32:10 - "I am the apple of my father's eyes"

CHAPTER 8
SAVING MY GRANDSON "KESHAWN"

When my first grandchild "Keshawn" was born on June 30, 2003, I was right there in the delivery room with my daughter "Ekia" coaching her to push harder, at the excitement of welcoming my grandson into the world, took me back to a place I'd been since my youngest daughter was born eleven years prior.

I remember seeing everything in that delivery room, as though it was yesterday. Once he exited from my daughter's womb, the doctor called out, it's a boy. The nurses cut the umbilical cord, washed the little fellow off, wrapped him in his blanket and handed him over to me, saying "Congratulations, Grandma! Here is your new grandson. As I reached for him crying at the top of his lungs, rocking him and smiling from ear to ear, saying to him "welcome into the world, little man, I am your grandma," and I promise to take good care of you always.

As you all can probably imagine, I was devastated and not so thrilled, when I first learned that my daughter was pregnant, at 16 years old. I was a single mom with two daughters already, five years apart, buying a condo, like I told you all about earlier in Chapter I. I had a car note, along with miscellaneous expenses, and I averaged around 35,000 per year with lots of overtime, if needed. Like any ordinary mom, I assumed that my little angel was still a virgin, because she never brought any boys to the house to introduce them to me, nor did any call the house.

I drilled her about how could she do this to me, knowing well how I was struggling to provide for her and her baby sister. The reason why I got fixed was to ensure that I never had any more kids, and now you want to force me into it anyhow. I was worried that she wouldn't finish school. She stood firm in letting me know that it was her decision, her body and that she was having her baby, and she didn't have to live under my roof.

"She was right," it was her decision and her body, and it was on me, to find a way to deal with it, continue to love her, be there for her and make preparations for the new addition to our family.

I eventually started working a lot more of overtime, so that I could start saving for things the baby would need. When my daughter reached her last trimester, I took her down to social services to see if she qualified for public assistance and food stamps. We were told that by her still being a minor, she didn't qualify and I would be responsible for the full care of this child, until she reached 18 years old. The only thing she qualified for on her own was the W.I.C.S. which came in very handy over the years.

Once the little fellow arrived into this world, I accepted him, and fell in love with him as my very own son. He was like the son, I would never have, and this is what is meant by, "never say never," because "God" always has a plan, far beyond what we can see into the future.

Once he came home, I'd already bought a basinet for him that fit perfectly between my daughters' two twin beds, an extra dresser for him, the baddest car seat and stroller, by Eddie Bauer. I wanted him to be riding in style (LOL).

I became a very protective grandma, always wanting to know, whose house my daughter was taking him to, how long they'll be gone and staying on top of her with keeping up with all of his doctor's appointments. I wanted my daughter to go back and finish school, so I hired my mother to babysit. I would drop him off early before I went to work and picked him up in the afternoons, once I got off from work, accepting full responsibility, as if he was my son.

On a few different occasions, different family members would offer to babysit him over the weekend, in which we accepted, but little did they know they would be in for a rude awakening. "Keshawn" wasn't a typical baby, he would holler and scream to the top of his lungs for extended periods of time, for no reason, and once the caregiver got a sense of this, they'll be calling me or Ekia to come and get him as soon as possible. The screaming was too much for them. My daughters, my mother and myself, were the only ones' he allowed to keep him.

A year later, after his first birthday, I was selling my condo and relocating to Atlanta, Georgia. I was looking for a change of scenery and better living for my children, but my daughter "Ekia," didn't want to move there with us, so we made an agreement that she would allow me to take him with us, while she stayed and tried to get on her feet.

Once we were settled down there, I was able to find him an in-home childcare provider that was very good with children. It wasn't easy for her in the beginning, because he gave her a fit also. It was hard for me to depart from him each morning that I dropped him off, because he still would go through the motions, causing me to feel so sorry for him. However, once I returned in the afternoons, he was so excited to see me, holding out his arms for me to pick him up and hurry up, to get him out of there.

Eventually, he did get use to his routine of going there back and forth. It was during our stay in "Atlanta, GA," when his pediatrician discovered that he wasn't developing at the current age he should have been, and recommended that I contact this agency for children with delayed disabilities.

Once everything was set up, the teachers would come to see him at the babysitter's house, eventually, that's when it was discovered that he was "autistic." It explained a lot of things like why he started talking, walking and potty training later than an average child would.

When we moved back to DC, I got in touch with the right people to continue his treatments. It was a long process, because he had to be evaluated by several doctors' and treatment plans. Then when he was about 2 years old, he was accepted into one of the best schools for Children with Disabilities in S.E. DC. The school provided transportation to and from, free meals, and a team of speech and occupational therapists. They took the kids on great trips, in which I chaperoned on a few with my grandson.

Once he turned four years old, the school discharged him, because they felt that he was ready for head start. I am happy to say that he did exceedingly well in his 1st year, as far as being dropped off and not feeling afraid, interacting with other kids and knowing how to put his things away.

My grandson was my heart and joy, and I always wanted to keep him. I kept up with all of his school uniforms, supplies, doctors' appointments, and we were always on the go. I wanted him to experience having a good life. We went on family vacations once a year. I was always taking him sight-seeing to the museums where I worked. We ate at expensive restaurants; we were always going to the movies together; his favorite fast-food was KFC – for the macaroni and cheese. Whenever I visited family and friends, I would have him with me a lot. He looked forward to spending time with me outside of me working and him going to school, as I look forward to doing exciting and adventurous things with him.

Keshawn was 5 years old and was spending the weekend at my house, on that fatal night, when my husband "Kerry" had agreed to watch him, after he had just gotten off from work and I was on my way to my part-time job. Keshawn was asleep, when "Kerry" arrived, so when he had awakened sometime in the middle of the night, he probably assumed that I should've been the one there, not realizing we changed shifts. But once he discovered that no one was in the home, and he was all alone, that would've frightened any kid.

So on impulse, he didn't think about getting his coat, hat or putting on his shoes. He opened the door, which set off the burglary alarm, and he fled in only his P.J.'s and socks, in the middle of the night at 3 am in the freezing temperatures of only 20-something degrees. I don't know what told his little mind to go next door and knock on the next door neighbor's house, but "Thank God" they were home and up that time of morning to hear his little knock, as she described.

She said, he was trembling from the cold, crying and saying "they left me." She brought him inside, then located my cell number and called me, which was about 3 am. Once she informed me of this, she did assure me that he could stay there until I'd gotten off from work in the morning. I wish I'd accepted her offer, and then I wouldn't be sitting in a "federal" prison right now. But, I told her, I appreciated her offer, but I didn't believe he would be comfortable staying over a stranger's house, and that after a while, he might have started giving them a hard time, and that I would feel better coming to pick him up. So I abandoned my post and flew across town to do so, and from there, one thing lead to another, in which you read about in Chapter 3.

I rushed to my grandson's aid, as any mom probably would have done, in a panic, never realizing in a million years that it was going to end deadly. I regret that my grandson had to witness the entire episode unfold. He would've been a perfect witness for me, if only he could've talked clearly, but at the time, due to his autism disorder, he was dismissed as my witness, due to his autism disorder, is why he didn't realize he needed a coat, a hat and shoes to go outside.

A lot of people still aren't aware of this disorder, so I have done my own research and included some recent studies that have been reported.
One of the characteristics of autism, a neurological disorder that impairs communication, socialization and other behaviors, is rigidity. Autistic children can get fixed on anything – a piece of string, a spec of wall paint or a golden brown bear on grass

holding toilet paper with the words "Charmin Ultra Strong" in white letters above his head.

A recent study shows autism affects 1 in 91 children (up from 1 in 150) and 1 in 58 boys. It is the fastest growing developmental disability in the United States. Grace Baker Simpson is a freelance journalist and media-public relations consultant in Windsor, Connecticut. Reported in Heart and Soul: Feb/March 2010

USA Today, October 8, 2012 (Michelle Healy)
Nearly half of children with autism wander from safety
The problem can frighten parents and be deadly for children

The fear that overtakes a parent when a child wanders away is easily compounded when that child has an autism-spectrum disorder. A new study shows that such behavior occurs more often than in other kids, and the hazards can be significant.

In a sample of 1,200 children with autism, 49% had wandered, bolted or "eloped " at least once after age 4; 26% went missing long enough to cause concern. Only 13% of 1,076 siblings without autism had ever wandered off at or after age 4, when such behavior typically becomes less common, finds the study in today's *Pediatrics*. Among children with autism who went missing, 65% had close calls with traffic; 24% were in danger of drowning.

"Elopement is one of the very few problems in autism that is life-threatening, says study author Paul Law, a pediatrician and director of the Interactive Autism Network Project (ianproject.com), a national autism database headquartered at the Kennedy Krieger Institute in Baltimore. "It is probably one of the leading, if not the leading, causes of death in children with autism."

Among other study findings:
- ➢ Elopement attempts peaked at age 5 for kids with autism.

- From 4 to 7, 46% of kids with autism bolted, vs. 11% of siblings. From 8 to 11, 27% did; from 12-17, 12% did.
- Children who wandered had more severe autism symptoms and had lower intellectual and communications scores than those who did not.
- The places kids bolted from most were their home or another's (74%), stores (40%) and schools (29%).

The risks associated with her daughter's elopement behavior led Alison Singer of Scarsdale, NY to install alarms on every door in her house. From ages 5 to 10, Jodie, now 15, would try to leave in the middle of the night in search of things, from the Chinese restaurant that served her favorite egg rolls to a book she read at a neighbor's two years before.

"It just got into her head that she wanted it, and she'd head out to get it," says Singer, president of the Autism Science Foundation, one of several groups that funded the study.

The federal government recently created a medical diagnostic code for wandering as a condition of autism, an important first step in efforts to get preventive services, says Singer.

To my grandson Keshawn,

    I love you so much. You are the best grandson, a grandma can have. I want you to know that I will always have your back and you can always talk to me about anything that's on your mind or bothering you. I'll always want to listen, no matter what it is about. I want you to always have a voice and to fear nothing but the Lord. You are loved and I am always here for you. I want you to always reach your goals, whatever that may be, and just know that you will be held accountable for your actions and choices and in order to be the best you have to be willing to go the extra mile.

I hope that you will always remember "happy" times we shared together, as I do. Always be willing to give from your heart, because sharing is a blessing from "God."

Lastly, my boy, lean on the ability of God to bring you success in your endeavors, because God promises not to let us down or abandon us or leave us alone. He is not slack or absent in the day of adversity. And he is ready to stand by us until death.

Love always,

your Grandma

Ecclesiastes 4:10 – For if they fall, one will lift up his fellow. But woe to him who is alone when he falls and has not another to lift him up

CHAPTER IX
FAMILY

I am very thankful and fortunate to have had a good choir by my side. Good family and friends that was my choir, they were with me when I had   fallen. I am not normally an aggressive person when it comes to defending myself, and it will bother me for the rest of my life so bad, that I took a life, even though I felt like I was within my rights.

We as human beings are fallible, like myself.

My mother always instilled in all five of her children good values that are essential for success. She's someone I always had great admiration for. My mother is one of the happiest people I know, no matter what hand she was dealt in life, she would pick herself up, dust herself off and keep going. She was also a wonderful stay-at-home mother who taught me and the rest of my siblings well.

Every one of my siblings, mom, uncles and aunt, played an important role in helping me to get through my time, in some form, shape or fashion. Let me tell you how starting with my "mom" who was always gifted with wonderful people skills.

"Mom, Cat," was never much of a traveler, even while we were growing up, or before me coming into this situation. So I didn't expect many visits from her, but she came about twice a year, until she became ill, and was diagnosed with Breast Cancer in 2012. She went through a series of treatments, until her last radiation treatment in August 2013, but came out of a remarkable recovery, and was rewarded with a certificate of completion. I couldn't have been more proud of her, and I want to give a special thanks to my sister, "Jacqueline," for taking off of work, for every treatment to be there by her side.

In 2011, I was approved for a partial scholarship through this non-profit organization, called "Our Place." I was responsible for the remaining balance, in which I couldn't afford to pay on prison salary, so I called my dear mom, and asked her if she would be able to help me with the remaining payments of sixty dollars a month for the next twelve months. I was honored that she agreed, then the payment coupons were sent to her each month to take over. Upon the last payment, I received my "Paralegal/Legal Assistant" certification. Thank you so very much Mom....

My sister "Jacqueline" is my mom's second child, we are almost 2 years apart in age, and she is not only my sister, but my best friend, in the whole wide world. Even before my down fall, we were always close at heart. There wasn't too much of anything that we both, don't feel comfortable talking about or sharing our innermost secrets. We've been through thick and thin together, in good ways, but I'm not going to go into detail, enlisting all those moments, because then it would take up the rest of this book (LOL).

After I was sentenced, I asked my sister to promise me something, and she said anything. I asked her to please bring my grandson to come and see me every visit that she comes, to ensure that he will never forget who I am. She told me she would, but also laid out to me that she doubted if he ever would, because he talks about me all the time, and certain places they would pass, he'll say to her, ma took me there before. She never knew this, but my eyes filled with tears upon this message. I am happy to say that nearly every visit, my sister has kept that promise.

For the 3-1/2 years that I was incarcerated at "Hazelton" prison, my sister, "Jacqueline," faithfully visited me once a month. There were times, I had to tell her to take a break next month, I'm okay, like for her Birthday month, and a couple of the brisk wintery cold months. But usually each time, she drove down, she'd bring someone different in the family, like my daughter, our childhood friend "Sharon," or "Denise," a different sibling or an ex-boyfriend, have rode along with her also.

My sister has acted as my personal secretary, my entire bid, I always needed her to go to some website and look up something for me, type up long motions for me, call different business places for me, order different things for me, like free catalogs, forward emails for me, and research certain information. The amazingly thing about my sister, if she got tired of me, she never said "no," she didn't have time or couldn't do it. Whenever, I called her on the phone, she never sounded like she didn't want to talk to me. She was always happy to hear from me, and anxious to tell me about what was going on at the time, with the family. In fact, she also typed this entire manuscript up for me. God Bless her soul (Right)….

My mother's third child is my brother "Tyrone," we are 6 years apart. This is the brother I told you about earlier, in Chapter IV that was just getting out of prison, the same year, I went in. Growing up we had our sibling rivalries like anyone else, but our family has always been close knit, and we all love one another very much, although we didn't always say it in words to one another.

My brother, "Tyrone," was always a go-getter, he loved fast money, expensive clothes and cars. He always landed nice jobs, working in hospitals, then he somehow got around the wrong crowd, and started going downhill slowly. After being in and out of jail for over 20 years, my brother said he finally woke up and learned his lesson, and he was never returning to drugs or jail again. I look at him now and I see a side, I never thought I would see, before leaving this earth. I'm seeing now a changed man, going on 5 years, and he has done a 360 turn around.

Once he got his self together, far as landing a decent job, he started sending me enough money to be comfortable with faithfully every month. He didn't have to worry about a place to live, because during his short period of incarceration this last bid, he had a long-time girlfriend, he maintained ties with, and now I am excited to tell you that a week before Christmas of 2013, he proposed to her. My brother has come to visit me a few times as well; he sends me cards on every holiday, because he didn't forget where he came from and remembers how important it is to receive mail. When I decided to take my "Day Care Assistant" course on the outside, he happily paid for the majority. I could go on bragging about all the great things he has done since turning his life around, but I'll leave the rest of the formalities at a standstill.

    My mother's fourth child's name is Glorine, but we all call her G.G., for short, she is the one I told you about earlier, that moved into my house to save it for me. I will always be indebted to her for this. G.G. and I weren't always as close growing up, because of our age difference, and different lifestyles.

My mother's fifth child is my brother, "Reggie." Reggie and I are a huge gap apart, 12 years to be exact. I remember growing up, I spoiled him more like a son, if I'd ever had one. I would take him with me to many places, once even to "Disney World," besides I was his oldest sister and I wanted to set examples for him, that he could always look up to me, and be there for him, if he needed me. But when I took this great big fall, I somehow feel like I failed him, although to this day, he's never told me so, but on the night that I was arrested, and brought out of the house in the handcuffs, he was standing outside, alongside my sister and daughter, and I could see the look of shame on this face.

During my brief period of incarceration, "Reggie," didn't have a lot of luck with his own place, nor place of employment. He either bounced back and forth between staying with my sister, "Jack," or my mom, until finally my mom's rental office, noticed that he was over staying and he had to leave immediately. Reggie likes to smoke cigarettes and drink, so when he would work, a great portion of his income would go towards that, causing him to go broke quick. His jobs would either run out or he'll get fired. So therefore, I understood why he could never send me any funds, but he did manage one time to help me out with one school payment, and I was grateful for that. He also wrote me more uplifting and encouraging letters, than my baby sister. Each letter was always short, brief and to the point, but the fact of the matter, is that he made time to do so, and that meant more to me than he'll ever know. A lot of people who have never been to prison, don't realize how much difference they can make in an incarcerated person's life, just by sending a simple note, card or writing a brief letter. He also added in each letter that he is praying for me and hoping for a positive result.

    Additionally, I have a half-sister, her name is "Crystal." Unfortunately, we didn't grow up together. My other siblings and I didn't meet her until our adulthood. But, she was just as supportive and by my side as well.

I have an Uncle also that stood faithfully by my side, from the beginning of my first court arraignment and his name is "Harmon." He is my father's only living brother left, and every time I'd see him at court with the rest of the family or whenever he came to visit me, I somehow got a vision that dad had sent him, and he was standing there in the gap for him. During this ordeal, he was a blessing to me in many ways. My sister would often tell me that he would often call her to see how I was doing and to check on the status of my appeal. In my opinion, I believe that I had always been his favorite niece, so sisters of mine's don't be jealous (LOL).

Family has always been very important to me. While in prison, I couldn't seem to stop worrying about all their welfare. Both my daughters had to learn to find their own way in the world, once I left, because I spoiled them both growing up. They each went through their own struggles out there, and there wasn't anything I could do to rescue them. It eventually came down to deciding to let God do what I could not.

    I prayed for my daughters and grandchildren around the clock. I trusted God for their souls, because I knew they were in the best of care. Placing my kids in God's hands gave me a measure of inner peace that was restored.

"Friends"

I am very excited about telling you about six amazing ex-coworkers that stuck by my side, just as close as family. At the time of my arrest, I had only worked at the National Gallery of Art for two years, so I'd like to think that I left an exceptional impact on each of these angels, that "God" blessed in my life, and to be honest with you, they stuck by my side closer than so-called friends, I've known half my life and cousins.

I'm sure you've heard the saying before, sometimes "God" sends people in your lives, for a "season, a reason or a purpose." I got blessed with all three. For the sake of protecting each of their privacy, I am only going to name each one by their first initial only.

Mrs. G is one of the truest and mature Christian women, I've ever known and she let me know that on several occasions, in comparing certain situations, we would discuss. She wrote to me faithfully for my entire five years, sometimes three or four times a month. She never skipped a month, we had an ongoing communication. It was fun being her pen-pal, because she kept me abreast on all the happenings on and off the job. We both stood in the gap of prayer for many of the co-workers, and both our family members. She never missed sending me a card, for every holiday occasion, even St. Patrick's Day. We stood on "God's" promises for so many things.

Next, I'd like to introduce you to Mrs. I, we shared a close bond also, and she never skipped a month in writing me either, in the entire five years. She also sent me cards for every occasion. She would also keep me abreast on everything that was happening on and off the job, her health, her family and achievements. She always found me bible scriptures that she would quote to me, at the end of every letter. She was genuinely concerned about me, and she also made sure that I had an obituary of every co-worker that had passed away, since I left there.

Next, I'd like to introduce you to "Mrs. V." One of "God's" anointed angels, indeed, and I often told her this. She also never skipped a month in writing me or sending me cards for every occasion, sometimes cards just because, to say I am thinking about you. She would give me the impression that she worked at the postal office as her second job, because she sent me cards, letters, and sometimes large envelopes of different email messages, funny or uplifting and encouraging, that required several postages, six or eight times a month. She was never lengthy in her letters or cards, always brief, and to the point, but the fact that she always made time for me, out of her schedule, tells me a lot, and speaks volumes to me. I've found a friend for life.

Next, I'd like to introduce you to Mr. R. I couldn't have been more honored, that "God," allowed him to remain by my side, so willingly and faithfully. He also never skipped a month in writing me and sending more than one card, on every holiday occasion. He made me feel like a queen in prison, because he added spice and romance to some of his letters that would put me in a twilight zone, so-to-speak (LOL). He helped me willingly on several of my school payments, and he purchased me Bible puzzles and Christian books throughout the year. He was the only one that visited me one time, while I was in federal prison, which was more than enough for me.

    Mr. R is a good man, but I feel confident in saying that he is the only man, that I have ever known my entire life, that is about as honest, realest and truest as they come, in a man. Any woman would be blessed to have him in their life. Let me elaborate to you what I mean. After I had lost at trial, and knew that I would be gone away for a long time, I informed him of this information, as I did each one of these ex-coworkers, and I didn't expect him to keep in touch with me for all those years, but if he chooses to, to please always be honest with me about everything to include any of his relationships. Because let's face it, there isn't anything I can do for you, from in prison, and he agreed that he would. He would also say whether he had feelings for them or not. I was a listening ear for him. Mr. R is also a supportive dad, not a dead beat one, just because he is no longer with their moms. He is a dedicated brother to his two sisters and loving and supportive son to his mom and dad, who are both still living and together. He also served our country in the military, for over a decade, and is the best culinary cook, I know. He has a bachelor's degree as well.

He never failed to amaze me yet, on several occasions, he told me, while he was writing me a letter on post at work, someone would see him, and ask him who is he writing and he'd say … a pen pal/ex-co-worker that use to work here, and they would be like, oh you're writing "Mozella," tell her I said hello; he was never ashamed to tell them he was writing me.

Mr. R's letters were always very long and detailed, and so were mine's, in return. We both enjoyed answering each other's letters. He also provided me with spiritual support, which he is also a Christian man. I could go on and on in describing this man, but I think I'll stop here and leave some room for the others. I love this man!

Next, I'd like to introduce you to Mr. D. Everyone use to think that he was my boyfriend at work, because we were so close, but we were just plain platonic friends, never dated, nor had sex, so let me clear the air on that. He was another good friend. Mr. D visited me faithfully the entire time I remained at CCA. He wrote me occasionally, but not as often as the others. He sent me funds, during the entire time, I was at CCA, but he eventually had to go out on disability, so he was no longer able to and I understood that. Mr. D had a lot of skeletons in his closet, and I'll leave it at that, but I told him also the same thing as I did with Mr. R, after I learned I would be going away for a long time. He, didn't hang with me the entire time, as did the others, but he'll still be forever my friend.

Lastly, I'll introduce you to an ex-coworker/boyfriend; his name is Mr. D also. I was fortunate to have two friends with the same first name and very similar character. Both of them have a heart of gold. Me and this Mr. D dated for several years, until we were no longer compatible and went our separate ways, but we still remained friends. Sadly, to say, I never told him that I had gotten married. He had to learn about it, through this unfortunate down fall of mines. I wouldn't have much blamed him, if he had run for the hills, but he didn't, he still remained by my side, and by both my daughters side, as well. They look up to him as a step-father still today. Every time they call him, because they are in a crunch, he is right there to dig them out, if he has it, just like they were his very own. He has helped me as well, during my incarceration, with school payments, mail orders and miscellaneous things. He did come and visit me once, which I was grateful to see him, after years, since I've left the county jail, where he did visit me there also.

I feel like I will always be indebted to him for life, because he even testified on my behalf, and that alone speaks volumes to me. I'll love him forever also.

There are two special ladies, I would like to acknowledge at this time also, they aren't ex-coworkers, but both childhood friends. I grew up with from elementary school until now. Denise and Sharon both stood by my side for the long haul, and never lost faith in me or doubted my actions, that fatal night. They both have visited many times and kept me encouraged. I love them both, as if they were my blood sisters.

I'm reminded of an old adage saying that someone once shared with me. "All that left me couldn't stay and all that stayed couldn't leave." Some people are seasonal blessings loaned to you to perform a purpose and when the season is up and the purpose completed, they will leave.

The people who really care about us will not throw our past mistakes back in our face. They refuse to utter the words, "I told you so." It was a hard lesson to learn and painful to accept, because no matter how good a person you were, not everyone in the world has you or your best interest of heart.

My Faith

"Yes," I was blessed beyond measure to have good family and friends, in my corner. Having a support system like this, allows one to get through his or her time much easier. There were numerous of times, I had to wrestle with those strongholds, the devil kept laying on me, but through faith and preservation I got through it. I could have kept crying out, "Lord," what am I going to do? Instead, I began to say, "I've not been given a spirit of fear!" "No weapon formed against me will prosper!"

Trials are not permanent, but the Word of God is. Second Corinthians 4: 17-18, saying, "Our light affliction, which is but for a moment, is working for us a far more exceeding and external weight of glory, while we do not look at the things which are seen, but at the things which are not seen. For the things which are seen are temporary, but the things which are not seen are eternal."

So whatever you're facing today, whatever you're going through, it's not permanent! The

Apostle Paul was left for dead, beaten and jailed on numerous occasions. But he said, "I thank my God that I always triumph in Christ Jesus" (2 Corinthians 2:14)

The devil was always trying to shift my focus away from God and his Word, especially in the midst of my adversity. I had to keep reminding myself that what I was going through wasn't permanent! God is faithful to perform his Word in your life…

I stayed focus on these things mainly (1) remembering that God is with me and wants to help me out of my trouble; (2) resisting fear, 2 Timothy 1:17; (3) realizing that God always has a way out, 1 Corinthians 10:13; (4) putting my faith to work, Mark 11:23-24; (5) maintaining the proper confession, Hebrews 10:23; and (6) always maintain a good attitude, James 1:2.

Following these actions, in faith will get you through the tough times, it did for me.

I am now going to give you a little overview about myself. I am a very tender-hearted person that always cares deeply about the hurts of others. I wish that I had sought help or advice from someone, before this big fall. I always tried to maintain a positive enthusiastic attitude, treating co-workers on any job I had ever worked, with respect and dignity. I was honest and dedicated to my work, following company policies and procedures, following directions and standards of professionalism.

I am a very dedicated and respectful individual whose sole purpose was to work hard as I could for my children. I feel ashamed for the stupidity that I have gotten myself caught up in.

I've always been one that takes things as they come without getting all nervous and upset about them. I've always had a tolerance for risk, "you aren't going anywhere in life, unless you take risks." I am a friend to the end, that's how I've always been, even in relationships that ended. I've always tried to stay friendly and civil as long as the other person wanted to.

I give my heart away too easily, to the things of the world.

Until that fatal night, I'd always had self-control. I've always been a hard working dependable person, who was not quick to anger and showed pride in my ability to find ways to get out of problems without using force or violence.

Psalms 126:5 – "They that sow in tears shall reap in joy."

CHAPTER 10
AND, SO MY JOURNEY BEGINS IN PRISON

In many areas of life, we have to adapt, sometimes to unwelcomed realities. We have to move beyond asking "why," to discerning "what now?" God never leaves us in a place where grace cannot sustain us.

Luckily for me, during the long induration that I spent at the county jail, had eased my fears a great deal of all the horror stories I've heard from others or seen on television about it, before entering federal prison. I was finally transferred to prison about six weeks after being sentenced.

I didn't fret, because I knew in my heart that the "Lord" almighty was with me. Upon entering the compound, there were several women, I'd already known from the county that greeted me, and of course, the nosey ones' who wanted to know how much time, I was given.

I'd done made up my mind, right after sentencing that I wasn't going to be claiming that entire sentence. Since it was broken down, I would only be claiming the murder conviction, because if my firearm had been registered in the District of Columbia, I wouldn't have been convicted on those offenses. My firearm was legally mines, but only in the state of Maryland.

It was July 2010, when I touched federal grounds. On my first night there, I came down with the worst migraine headache ever. I guess I'd become overwhelmed with trying to digest the reality of this being my home for the next decade or so. It was a painful reality to digest.

The scary moment didn't come all at once, I was still in faith mode. I knew who my "God" was, so I didn't panic, going to prison is something no one is mentally prepared for, but with "God" on your side, who can be against you.

As the months went on, I found me a job, working on the outside compound mowing grass, with these 1990's lawn mowers in the spring and summer months and shoveling snow in the cold wintery months. I did that for about a year, until it became too much on my back, for only $19.20 a month, they worked us like slaves in a cotton field.

I'd already started programming myself, while working this job, within this years' time, I'd probably taken at least fifteen classes by then. I was on a serious mission, to obtain as much education as I possibly could, with all the time, I had on my hands, now was the time to do it.

By the middle of September 2013, I'd taken at least sixty courses, including three correspondence courses that my family and friends had all pitched in together, for the monthly tuitions. I would make a list of about six or seven people, and then calculate a reasonable amount, if each could contribute diligently. I'll write them a letter stating the need, the course and where to send the payments, so they wouldn't think that I wasn't jiving them out of extra money. I'd never been one to ask for money to this degree, until coming to prison, because I always had my own, but circumstances had changed and I was following what 1 Peter 5:5 says, God gives to the humble and resists the proud, and I can truly say with sincerity that not one that I'd asked turned me down. They all were more than willing.

God continued to keep propelling me to the next level, in everything he saw me putting forth the effort to learn. On all my correspondence courses, I made the Dean's list and succeeded with honors.

In early January 2013, a list had come out for a new "Entrepreneurship" class that was starting soon. I signed up, as so many others had, not knowing that an entrance exam was required in order to get into this class. A list was compiled together, with everyone's name on it that had signed up, consisting of about sixty of us.

The education coordinator had scheduled for everyone to come in one particular morning to take the entrance exam, there was no warning or preparation time, but once all was seated, we were told that in order to be put into the class, you had to pass it. He said that 25 questions were "Reading and Comprehension and 25 problems of "Algebra." At the mention of algebra, my head dropped and I said to myself, "I'm done." I'm going to be honest with you all, I'd never be good at "Algebra." It was always my weakest subject, an in order to get through it in high school, I cheated my way out.

I'd set myself up to fail this time. Once our test booklets were passed out, we were given scratch paper, then timed for 25 minutes at 25 problems. I'd said to myself, I'm not going to waste these people time, trying to figure out these problems that I know I don't know how to do. So I went down the entire test guessing every answer within ten minutes. Then once that test was completed, we were given the other test, which also was timed for 25 minutes.

Now, I did take the time to answer all those questions, to the best of my ability.

As everyone was leaving from the Education building, people were asking, how you think you did? When asked of me, I told them quickly, "failed," because I haven't a clue about "Algebra," and I guessed every single answer. They laughed, and said "oh, don't be so hard on yourself," you never know. Well, about a month later, we were all called back who had passed the test. He said, everyone that is seated back in here has passed their test and can be placed in the first "Entrepreneurship" class. I said to myself, is this a dream "God," I actually passed that test. God, all I can say, is nobody but you, and "Thank you, Jesus" for your favor being upon me. This course gave us nine credited hours, through a Community College the prison had a contract with.

I'd always been passionate about education. I'm delighted to say that I passed this course also with all "A's'." Nobody but "God."

Prison will teach you patience and perseverance, because everywhere you went consisted of long lines, for the dining hall, pill line, commissary, holiday events, and lines for getting sanitary napkins, toilet paper and getting stripped out after having a visit.

I didn't like how all our under garments had to be white. In the free world, I would never wear white panties, while my cycle was on. I discovered early into my time, that prison is a money-maker. These women would steal everything and anything that wasn't nailed down. Whatever you wanted out the kitchen, the workers set their prices, and if you wanted it, you paid them with commissary items or having the money put into their books. In the laundry department, since we were only allowed new panties, socks and bras once a year, if you wanted any of these in-between the year, whatever laundry worker was hustling, you'll go to them for the hook-up. Commissary prices were ridiculous for dollar items you'd get on the streets. "Yes" God had brought me into captivity but only as a result of my sin, and the fact that he had a purpose for my life, other than the one I was pursuing. My sin created a separation from God, and in order to heal this relationship, God had to take me into captivity, cleansing me of my sin and restoring me back to himself.

Now, God has my full attention, but this was his plan all along. I understand that sin has consequences, I had broken the law and I had to face my punishment, and as another result, I learned to make the best out of a bad situation, trusting that "God" would do something wonderful with my time. Sometimes, adapting ourselves is the most faithful response we can make.

When I was first incarcerated, I went through a mental and emotional trauma. Then on top of that, the years the judge had given me, all that time scared the heck out of me, prompting me to seek God, in an intense way. I believe that God had purposes he wanted me to fulfill, before setting me free again, and so he could get me prepared for my future assignment.

While in prison also, I made up my mind that I was going to do my time, living a Christ-centered lifestyle, which meant that I was going to be total dependent on God. The way I worked this out, was every morning before starting my day, I would seek God through Bible-study, prayer and meditation. The more I did this for years straight, it became a routine. I was disciplining myself in order to be successful for the rest of my life. I wanted to be able to say, that I did my time wisely and smart. Always studying and growing both in God's Word, and educational. I looked at my incarceration as time spent going back to school.

Just as the seasons in nature change, so do the seasons in our lives. Our circumstances never stay the same for long.

For the first couple of years of my incarceration, my mind was tormented day and night and the only time I slept was out of exhaustion. I'd begun to lose hope. I learned to live one day at-a-time. I learned to depend on "God" to see me through each day, sometimes, minute by minute.

On the warmer and hot days, when we could go outside, I'd walk around the track yard, doing my laps and praising and worshipping the" Lord" in the midst of the battle, singing either "Thank you Lord" for everything you done for me, "Jesus," you are the center of my joy or "Praise the Lord for your mercy endures forever." He was faithful to come and flood my mind with his peace.

In the summer of 2012, we were finally able to purchase MP3 players, which would be an enhancement to doing a lot of our time. I got mine immediately, downloading only all gospel songs. My first song was, "I smile," by Kirk Franklin, and I'd play that song about 20 times back-to-back, increasing my walking speed on the track field. Those lyrics really connected to my heart, allowing me to speak to God from the depth of my spirit. I quickly learned that "Satan" can't stand in the presence of God and when I began to praise the Lord, his favor shined on me.

In spite of my circumstances, like "David," I remembered "God's" power and mercy and singing of them encouraged me to go on. The years I spent in prison, turned out to be a blessing to me, because I yielded to Jesus, and he used me to be a blessing to other inmates.

If someone had come to me, when I was a teenager and told me that I would be sentenced to twenty in prison for murder, I would've told them they were out of their damn mind. My life was promising as far as I could see, before I went off a cliff like "Thelma and Louise" and ended up in left field. I never would've foreseen that day coming.

You all, I'm sure have heard the saying before, "warning comes before destruction," and a haughty spirit before a fall."

There is a "right suffering" and a "wrong suffering." In 1 Peter 3:14, it says, "but in case you should suffer for the sake of righteousness, you are blessed." In verse 16, he exhorts us to live in such a way that we make sure our conscience is entirely clear and in verse 17, he goes on to say, for it's better to suffer unjustly for doing right, if that should be God's will, than to suffer "unjustly" for doing wrong.

So my suffering was not a hopeless suffering, but a suffering that actually produced hope, because I could see changes throughout the transition.

These were not always big changes, but the Lord always kept me from not giving up. Just when I thought I couldn't stand the pain any longer, he would come through with a special blessing that would let me know that he was there all the time watching over me.

I knew that God's grace and mercy kept me from seriously getting into a lot of fights; I only had one that happened one week before reaching my 5-year sentence. This nearly 300 pound devil thought she could bully me, punched me dead in the mouth, busting my lip, I broke loose from there, leaving her begging for me to stop hurting her. I came out the winner, gaining a lot of respect, for so many I'd surprised. "God," kept my hormones from letting me down, causing me not to want to experience the lesbian lifestyle, in order to fit in, losing myself, self-respect and becoming addicted to someone else's pills.

I am so grateful to the Lord and still in awe of how he kept me. Although I did not have those kinds of problems, I still had to wrestle with the devil, every now and then.

I managed to pretend to be happy, most of the times, because the greater one was living in me and pulling me through each day. Yet like so many people, I pretended that everything was fine, especially every time my family came to visit me or I talked to them on the phone. We human beings pretend for the benefit of others, not wanting them to know about our misery.

I know that God can't deliver us from everything, for some things we have to live with, but as long as you know that he walks with you, he will sustain you also. Sometimes "God" has to take away from you, in order to get your attention. We all fall down, but we can get back up again, like "Donnie McClurkin" sings, it best. Prison is the place, where your faith is tested!

"God's," got an assignment for me, so right now, I am where he needs me to be. I've chased after man, life, material things, now it was time to chase after "God." Everything is meant to be. I know it's an experience that I needed to have, if God was putting me through it.

I've gone through a lot of sad crying periods in there, wishing I had packed up my good sense and left him with everything, but the power of my faith pulled me through each day. I refused to let this crisis steal my joy and keep me from pressing forward, not as long as I was alive and still breathing, there is hope for me to still be all God created me to be.

To say, I've hit a turbulence in my life is an understatement. One minute you are happy and filled with contentment doing just fine. You have a great job, healthy children, and you are feeling blessed. My life took a temporarily plunge, no doubt!

While in prison, I discovered that I wasn't the only one that had suffered at the hands of a man for "Domestic Violence." I wasn't the only one who had dealt with tough issues of this matter. For me, it was very refreshing to share my story; anyone who asked what I was in for, I told them truthfully with no shame, because somebody else might have went through a similar situation. Conversely, as I heard their stories, and experiences of others, I too, was enlightened by the simple fact that I was human. From this ordeal, it taught me to never judge people without knowing their story first, or walking in their shoes.

God wants us to praise and thank him while we are in the wilderness of life as well! As on the mountain top, because what we say during trouble times, helps determine how long, we will be trapped in it. Remember my people, if you love God, you can count on him for anything you need. Sometimes God may lead us into troubled waters to deepen our trust in him.

It's been an eye-opening experience on many levels, but what has surprised me the most is witnessing how so many women wanted to be men, and how many women actually looked like men. I was always so naïve to this sort of stuff, and on the streets they were fooling me a lot of times, without me realizing it, and age ain't a factor. They get caught in bed with one another, and have no shame about it. They'll dating one this day for a period of time, then another one comes along, steals their heart away, and then they drop that one like a hot potato, still having to have to live with them on the same unit, with no shame. These women don't have anything on a man, because at least a man tries to hide his confrontation of both women meeting.

Some inmates were playing crazy and acting bizarre, just to get on crazy pills to jump start their social security checks upon release, but that was of my least of worries because according to Proverbs 3:14-15, wisdom is better than all the money in the world and more precious than jewels.

In other words, I needed all of my senses, understanding and tools working properly, like I entered prison with, to ensure long life, riches and honor upon my return back to society, that will be all anew to me.

To have wisdom is far incomparably better than anything a person could ever want (Proverbs 3:15). Wisdom brings pleasantness and peace and I needed both in order to do my time well (Proverbs 3:17).

As I would watch many of these women over the years, they reminded me of Jeremiah 4:22, they are wise to do evil, but to do good they have no knowledge and know not how. Most hadn't even the slightest clue that their chastisement would continue until it had accomplished its purpose, as so with me.

A lot of these women had fancy material things before coming to prison, and lost it all, but God Word says that if you choose to build with things the world has to offer, your house will be destroyed. I went to extremes to cut myself off from people, who could steer me in the wrong direction or interfere with my walk with God.

Everybody needs a trusted friend, who you can talk to, while in this place, I had a few, I can count on one hand.

I took an evaluation of the people I was surrounded by and I realized that because I am a good listener, many people came to me with their troubles. I am a problem solver by nature. There were a few that always complained, and it felt like it was never anything positive coming from them. There was unhappiness and negativity in every story they told. These people were draining my energy.

Then there were the compulsive and unnecessary liars that had their own stories.

During the time I spent in prison was much easier than I thought it would be, because it housed anywhere from five hundred fifty to eight hundred inmates at the most, and the inmates practically over-ruled all the rules. Let me give you some examples of what I mean: The inmates knew what correctional officers' enforced the rules, and which ones didn't. So things were never consistent. Sometimes we'll get shake down for about a week straight, after leaving the cafeteria, then back to the usual where you could come out with whatever you wanted. Now during the hours of 8 am – 3:30 pm, we are supposed to be in full uniform including your boots, if you didn't have a soft-shoe pass. I'd sprained my knee one time that allotted me a shoe pass for like 3 months, after it had long expired. I was still getting away with it for nearly a year, with no attempts of being stopped and asked whether or not I had one. Some got away with wearing even their flip-flops or P.J.s on the compound, contraband clothing, that some correctional officer's confiscated and some didn't. Mostly, the only times we got decent meals, were for Thanksgiving, Christmas, Holy Meals, Memorial Day, and 4th of July. The other meals we were supposed to be served according to BOP menu, was downhill, because the kitchen workers stole all the main ingredients, like the shredded cheese, butter, shredded chicken, ground beef or chicken tenders. These items would have to be replaced with something else. Also, it wasn't mandatory if one worked or not, as required of other FCI prisons. We didn't have to wear our shirts tucked inside our pants, as other FCI's is required. Normally, we were supposed to be out of bed by 7:30 am, beds made, but a lot followed that rule, and a lot didn't because it wasn't enforced much neither.

    A lot of women liked it here, because there was just no structure. There was always a big turnover with the staff, and administrators.

People were always complaining about the poor medical treatment they received, and the long extensive periods they had to wait before getting back out to their next follow-up visits to an outside specialist. I was blessed extremely, that I never had to stand and wait in the longest pill lines I'd ever seen to get their prescribed medicines. Every once in a blue moon, I'll go along with a friend of mine and wait for her, or push her in the wheelchair, when she became temporarily disabled. But, she knew I didn't like going over there and didn't ask too often. I'd let her know that it would be best if she asked someone else who had to go there as well.

Exodus 14:13-14: "The Lord will fight for you and you shall hold your peace and remain at rest."

CHAPTER 11
ALL IS REVEALED

My Appeals process didn't get started until sometime in early 2011. I learned that I was assigned to a public defender, by the name of Mr. Thomas Engle. After having my sister research him on the internet, and receiving shortly afterwards, a bio from him, I had an idea of who he was and his background in law and how many appeals he had prevailed on. So I figured, I would be in good shape. I had a qualm, maybe not, and that intuition came after seeing his address where he was located. He was in the exact same building and floor where my trial Attorney was located.

From my experience, in these sorts of things (meaning my case) men have a tendency to stick together, so I was afraid that a conflict of interest would occur, but still remained hopeful, for a positive outcome.

This Attorney handled my Appeals for nearly a year-and-a-half. During this time period, all our correspondence was via mail, and we would exchange our emails through my sister, as most Attorneys don't like sending direct emails, on "BOP" website, because they're being read. I was doing a lot of research on my case, so I was always sending him different cases that related to mine, then he'd send me his input back, as to whether he could use them or not.

In August 2012, I received notice from Mr. Engle, that it hurt him to be able to tell me that after long and hard research, there wasn't anything he could do for me, and was therefore filing an "Ander's Brief" to the Courts and withdrawing as my Attorney. I had no idea what an "Ander's Brief" was, so I showed it to a good friend of mines and asked her what did he mean by an "Ander's Brief."

She told me that when an "Attorney" files this, it pretty much means that you have lost, based on the fact that they couldn't find any merits in your favor. I was like really, are you serious? She was like "yes," I'm so sorry, the next step, is for you to file your "2255."

I was like ah shucks, now I'm going to have to see if my family can afford to hire "Craig" for me. Craig Cosarelli, is an ex-felon/paralegal that a lot of inmates hire, who can afford his services to do their 2255 motions.

About a month later that friend who told me this, was transferred to another prison. In September 2012, I received a letter from the Courts, informing me that Mr. Engle had finalized my appeal, and they were giving me 14 days to respond, as to whether or not I agreed, and if not an explanation, it didn't have to be in motion form, it could be written as a letter.

I felt like at this point, this would be my last shot, on whether or not I would prevail on my appeal, and with such a short period of time to work with. I knew I had to put together something quick, so I went inside my room, and fell to my knees, praying to the "Father," Lord, I don't know what to write and how to say it, but please let it be your will, that whatever I write, will be received by the Courts. (Amen).

I ended up writing a two or three page letter, citing cases and pointing out again how my case was self-defense. I mailed it off, within the time period, and left it in God's hand.

Three months later, in January 2013, I received another letter from the Courts, informing me they had accepted my motion and they were withdrawing Mr. Engle and appointing me another Attorney to take another look at my appeal. I was like "yes," thank you, "Jesus." This would be the second of my miracles and the beginning of God working his will for my life.

A couple of weeks later after this notice, I received a letter of introduction from my new appointed counsel, Mrs. Barbara E. Kittay, Esquire. I was so elated that I finally had a woman's eyes to look into my appeal. The Appeal's Court gave her 90 days to file my brief, and the government had 30 days thereafter.

She went on to tell me further in her introduction letter, that Mr. Engle had sent her my transcripts from the trial and other records, and she had begun her review to determine what issues, I may have on appeal. She also added that the Court of Appeal had rejected Mr. Engle's Ander's brief (which as you may know, is a brief that says he sees no valid issues that he would raise), which suggests also that the Court of Appeals would like another attorney to take a look.

Then she went onto giving me a full detail, of all of her qualifications to represent me. What brought tears to my eyes instantly, is when I got to the line, with her also telling me, in thirty years, I have handled dozens of appeals, nearly all successful.

Nevertheless, she believed that her experience provided me with the opportunity to have my case evaluated by someone who understands both sides of criminal prosecution and can more carefully scrutinize potential errors by the prosecution and the court. Also, since Mr. Engle has always been a defendant's attorney, and she had nearly always been a prosecuting attorney, I was getting both viewpoints, to scrutinize my record for errors.

In closing, she acknowledged that she knew I had been waiting already a very long time, and it still would take time to complete, and she hoped that I could remain patient. She said, that from time to time, we may speak by telephone, but mostly we will communicate by mail, and in the meantime, I could feel free to write her anytime.

Next, I had my sister, "Jacqueline" call to introduce herself to her, as my sister, and go-in-between advocate on my behalf, via email and phone. Once she got back to me, she said "Moe," you are so right, God is moving. Ms. Kittay says she can't make any firm promises, but she will do everything she can to help you. So let's pray that God uses her to show his glory.

About a month later, I received an email from my sister via my attorney, indicating that she hoped to file a brief next week, and listing what the issues would be. Sure enough that following week, she was sending me a copy of the brief, she had filed with the Courts, and now we wait for the government to respond. Generally, the Court grants them 30 days for a response. We will have 10 days to reply, and then we wait for the Court. She added that she would send me a copy of the government's brief, as soon as it was received.

Once I received a copy of the government's brief, and the reply she filed on my behalf, then she said, now we wait to see whether the Court will hear argument, which will mean that it is concerned about the conviction, based on an issue we have raised.

After I reviewed both briefs, I'd write down every case law, each used, and then go down to the law library and look up these cases and print them out. I was interested in knowing what each detailed, relating to mine.

In between waiting on the Court's response, I wrote a letter to my Attorney, sometime in May, asking questions just out of curiosity, if I didn't prevail on oral argument, would she be able to represent me in my "2255" motion as well. She wrote back, indicating that it is way too early for me to be planning a "2255" proceeding, and I should not worry about fees, because the Court likely will continue to appoint counsel for me, free of charge. Second, she went on to answering other questions, I had included, indicating my questions are most interesting, and she was glad I was reading the cases cited in the briefs. As you are now aware, she said, many cases have facts similar to yours, and for that reason, we can hope that the judges will grant argument, so we have an opportunity to persuade them of our position.

The following month in June 2013, I received a letter from her, indicating that she was writing with "Good News." The court of appeals had granted oral argument and was requesting her availability from September to November. She went on to say that this is good news, because the court would not schedule argument unless it was interested in the issues we have raised (if it were not interested, it would decide the case on the papers alone).

This would be my *third miracle in the court happening. She said, I don't have exact figures, but I would imagine that no more than 10% of cases are granted argument, most are decided on the papers alone.

Now as you can probably imagine, I had to be on pins and needles throughout the entire summer wondering about what the outcome would be. Since I had now made it this far in the game, I put on my helmet of faith and trusted in "God," to continue working behind the scenes on my behalf. I knew in my heart that he hadn't brought me this far to leave me now.

I received my next letter dated September 3rd, informing me that the calendar for October arguments had been released, and we are scheduled for 9:30 am on Tuesday, October 8, 2013.

After the argument, I will send you a detailed letter, summarizing the proceedings, giving you my impressions of whether our arguments were received favorably by the three-judge panel. She ended, by saying, I hope this letter finds you well, and satisfied that your case is finally moving forward. (Indeed, I was, and thanking and giving God the glory at the same time).

A month prior to my scheduled argument date, I began my fasting. I fasted two days each week, back-to-back, normally it would be on Tuesday and Wednesday. I chose "Tuesday," because that is when my argument would be heard.

On the last couple of days prior to that day, I switched my days to that Monday and Tuesday. That "Monday," I was joined with family and friends fasting together with me, on my behalf. I had stressed to them all, that my case was a tough one, and that plates would need to be turned down, all day from sunrise to sunset, and everyone was on board. My sister later admitted to me, how hard it was for her and how she ended up with a terrible migraine headache that evening. I said, I can only imagine, but thank you so very much and tell all the others also, "thanks a million." Much thought on prayer had gone up for me, by many people concerning my appeal.

Finally, my moment of fate, was going to be decided on, and had arrived. The attendees on my side were my sister Jacqueline, my daughters, and my Uncle Harmon, and on "Kerry's" side was just his mom. I learned later that afternoon from my sister, how she thought it had went, and that the prosecuting Attorney, Mr. Snyder was there, but sat in the back of the Court, because he wasn't allowed to say anything, just listen. I was told by my sister also, to phone my Attorney, so that she could go over all the details with me.

In our phone conversation, she told me the Judges were on our side for different reasons. They had seen how my trial Attorney was not performing efficiently, and they were very harsh about him. Trial counsel's preparation for and performance at trial, was so deficient, that I was deprived of my right to counsel. The judges seemed to be open minded and fair.

They requested that she file three code 23-110 motions and forwarded to Judge Jackson. The first would be a motion to hold my appeal in abeyance, pending the resolution of a motion in the Superior Court. The second was to vacate orders dated August 13, 2010 and July 26, 2011, each denying relief under DC Code 23-110; for reasons the Court did not appoint me a new counsel or schedule me an evidentiary hearing. They had treated my letter as a motion and denied the request as "vague and conclusory." The third motion would be to vacate my sentence and judgment, and also requesting that the Court schedule a hearing to determine whether the defendant was denied the effective assistance of counsel, and whether, as a result, her conviction should be vacated and a new trial ordered.

Since I have nothing to hide, and its public record, I am going to give you full details of all that was discovered at oral argument hearing.

The defendant intends to show, at a hearing on this motion, numerous examples of trial counsel's deficient preparation and trial performance, including but not limited to the following:

(A) Although the defendant qualified for representation under the Criminal Justice Act (D.C. Code § 11-2601, *et seq.*), and the court initially appointed an experienced Public Defender, appellant's family was approached in the hallway outside arraignment court by an investigator employed by counsel, who solicited the representation, in violation ethical standards. *Cf.* D.C. Bar Ethical Rule 7.1(d) ("No lawyer or any person acting on behalf of a lawyer shall solicit or invite or seek to solicit any person for purposes of representing that person for a fee paid by or on behalf of a client ... in the District of Columbia Courthouse, on the sidewalks on the north, south, and west sides of the courthouse, or within 50 feet of the building on the east side").

(B) Counsel presented the defendant to testify before the grand jury, even though her claims of self-defense were well-known to the government, and no advantage was gained from allowing the government to question her, in detail and without counsel present, particularly where counsel may have and should have known, at the time, that he might have to present her testimony at trial.

(C) Counsel waited until the day of trial to file what he claimed was a necessary motion to suppress the defendant's statements to the police;

(D) Counsel failed to pursue the identity of the police officer(s) who heard (and recorded in police records) the defendant's prompt claim of self-defense ("[h]e was trying to kill me, so I shot him"). When the government informed counsel, in a discovery letter, that "no police witness could recall the statement," he did not further demand an appropriate remedy, or in any way inquire into circumstances that could have provided a basis for admission of the statement, or to obtain a stipulation. Counsel did not demand that the government provide the witness or stipulation, under *Brady v. Maryland*, 373 U.S. 83 (1963), or to seek the court's assistance in securing information critical to the core of the defendant's affirmative defense.

(E) Counsel did not argue for the admission of this critical claim of innocence, under the "rule of completeness." *Samad v. United States*, 812 A.2d 226, 233 (D.C. 2002) ("When part of a statement has been admitted in evidence, the rule of completeness allows a party to seek admission of other parts or the remainder as a matter of fairness").

>In application in criminal cases, the rule of completeness is typically implicated when the prosecution selectively introduces only the inculpatory portions of a statement made by the defendant. Although the decision with respect to admission of omitted parts falls within the sound discretion of the trial judge upon request *must* admit additional portions that "concern the same subject and explain the part already admitted."

Henderson v. United States, 632 A.2d 419, 426 (D.C. 1993) (emphasis in original), *quoting Warren v. United States,* 515 A.2d 208, 210 (D.C. 1986).

(F) Counsel either did not notice or did not appreciate the significance of some or all of the information contained in discovery materials that identified the following of <u>decedent's</u> prior violent acts:

(i) a 1982 arrest in D.C., for assault;

(ii) a 1982 arrest in D.C. for destruction of property, carrying a pistol without a license, carrying an unregistered firearm, and unlawful possession of ammunition;

(iii) a 1985 arrest in Forestville, Maryland for battery;

(iv) a 1985 arrest in Prince Georges (P.G.) County, Maryland, for assault with intent to murder (AWIM);

(v) a 1990 arrest in P.G. County for the battery of Shonnell Jackson, the mother of the decedent's child;

(vi) a 1990 arrest in D.C. for disorderly conduct;

(vii) a 1990 arrest in D.C. for murder in the second degree (resulting in a conviction for assault with intent to kill). Counsel either was not aware of this case, or he confused it with the 1985 AWIM in Maryland; in any event, he appears not have understood that this was decedent's *second* arrest for murder.

(viii) a 1998 arrest in P.G. County for assault; and

(ix) a 1999 arrest in P.G. County for assault and weapon possession.

(G) Counsel appears not to have investigated the circumstances of these arrests, in order that he might present testimony critical to the defendant's claim of self-defense.

(H) Counsel failed to make a record of these prior violent acts, for effective review, on appeal, of the extent to which the defendant was prejudiced by the absence of this evidence.

(I) Counsel did not appear to know the correct rules and did not argue for the admission of the decedent's prior acts of violence, *to wit*, that they are admissible in homicide cases, whether or not known to the defendant:

> There is no question that the accused may present prior acts of violence committed by the victim and known to the accused to support a self-defense claim, as "such evidence is relevant to the reasonableness of the accused's fear of the victim." But in

homicide cases, an accused may also present evidence of a victim's prior acts of violence even if unknown to the accused to show that the victim was the first aggressor.

(J) The record is replete with examples of trial counsel's limited understanding of the rules of evidence and procedure, well-documented for presentation at a hearing on this motion.

(K) Counsel did not object when, in closing argument, the prosecutor untruthfully and improperly argued that the defendant had not claimed self-defense at the time of her arrest (when "she had the chance"), arguing instead, that she had fabricated the defense at trial, when, in fact, the prosecutor knew that the defendant promptly and consistently had made claims of self-defense and that he (the prosecutor) had argued vigorously for their exclusion.

After reading all this myself, and most of it, I didn't have a clue about, the holy spirit prompted me to read Jeremiah 33:3, "Call to me and I will answer you, and will tell you great and hidden things that you have not known."

*This would be my fourth miracle happening in the Courthouse.

Wait on the Lord, be of good courage and he shall strengthen your heart. Psalm 27:14. David grew into "a man after God's own heart," by waiting on the Lord (Acts 13:22).

1. After learning what the prosecutor had done, to say I was astonished is "an understatement." This man had belittled me in court each time, until the very end; I never thought I would see recompense being doled out from him; this man acted like he was above the law, but there was judgment. Sooner or later, every sin will be exposed and

paid for, an evil dictator fails, and a wrong is rectified. According to Proverbs 19:9, a false witness shall not be unpunished and he that speaks lies shall perish.

2. I think it is extreme for prosecutors to go through cheating, just to assure a conviction. I think it is a poisonous corruption of a system designed to protect the innocent at the risk of occasionally letting the guilty walk free. Further, I also believe that if a police officer is willing to cheat, they're just as dangerous as a defendant, he's trying to convict. These people have no conscience.

3. God saw way down the road that this day would come. He had a plan that encompasses far more than we could ever think or imagine. Oh, but I'm here to share with you that God heard my cry and came to my rescue.

4. God arranged my days to connect with the right people, when it was time for my appeal to go up.

Keeping some measure of hope, meant keeping some faith in the system. I've almost lost anyone I once had, because I've been framed, rail-roaded as just another guilty convict to an overzealous prosecutor. It hadn't been easy letting go of freedom in life, something that had been a part of me for 43 years.

I had to convince myself on many occasions, when things were looking bad for me, refuse to be discourage or angry "Mozella," and instead take a deep breath and tell yourself that "God" is still in control and that somehow everything is going to work out better than I ever dreamed.

Psalms 62:5 – "My soul, wait thou only upon God; for my expectation is from him."

CHAPTER 12
THE WAITING GAME

Prayer: Lord I pray in your infinite wisdom and power, you work behind the scenes to prepare all things for just the right time. Teach me to wait well and to trust you to know when the fullness of time has come. Teach me, Lord, the disciplines of patience, for to wait is often harder than to work.

Let's look at Romans 4:18-22, in this passage, we see Abraham waiting for his miracle to come through. The devil was assaulting him with doubt and unbelief. We can imagine the mental state he must have been in, thoughts pounding against his mind telling him that God was not going to come through.

The devil kept sending people in my path telling me about how the government had denied them for almost nine months, one would say, another a year. Her attorney had even put in for her to go out on an appeal bond also, and it was denied, and now she is down to one year to the door, before going home.

Sure they kept prolonging with me, but I knew this was all a part of my test too. I could hear the devil laughing each time he thought he won, and he could keep on as far as I was concerned. I'm still trusting in the Lord, to bring me across the finish line.

On October 10, 2013, my Attorney filed an order with Judge Jackson informing him on all the findings in my appeal. It would be staying pending resolution of the 23-110 motion in the Superior Court, and that while the matter remains pending in the trial court, counsel for appellant shall advise the court every 3 months, with the first report due on January 10, 2014, as to the status of the proceedings in the trial Court.

I received a letter along with this order from my Attorney also, informing me that we're in good shape either way, if Judge Jackson grants the motion, I get a new trial, and if he denies the motion, it joins the rest of the appeal.

On October 21, 2013, I had received a letter from my Attorney informing me that Judge Jackson has issued an order that the government respond to our motion by December 13. She said he must be expecting that the U.S. Attorney's office will conduct an investigation, to respond in substance, rather than to reflexively deny our allegations. She expects, however, that the government ultimately will deny and contest the allegations, but the response will provide valuable information, as we press the ineffectiveness claim. I'll keep you informed of the progress.

The next letter came from my Attorney on December 16, 2013, informing this time, that last Friday, when it's response was due, the government asked for an additional sixty (60) days to respond. It represented that it had not even begun its review; she enclosed a pleading along with the letter, opposing the request. She added also that, it would do nothing to speed up the process, but our position now may inure to our benefit later, if they ask for even more time (either in the Superior Court or in the Court of Appeals).

She understood that it was disappointing for me to see another delay, but as you know, she said, it is all part of the process, and likely can't be changed.

On December 24th, I received this letter from my Attorney informing me that Judge Jackson granted the government's request for more time, over our objection, and if they asked again, she would ask for release pending appeal. Judge Jackson won't likely grant release, but then she would appeal that order for me and continue the pressure.

This time the government was given until Monday, February 10, 2014, to file a response. So there I was waiting again, and each day that passed seemed like a thousand years. The response, I received from my Attorney after reaching this date, was what we both had expected, the government answered back this time, and of course, they opposed against everything that we argued and denied the motion. So now, it goes back to the trial Judge, in which he will either side with them or me.

On March 20, 2014, I was paged to the counselor's office to receive an Attorney/Client phone call. I felt in my spirit, that if she was calling me, it had to be some measure of good news, and sure enough, as soon as I said, "Hello, Ms. Kittay," how are you doing? She said, I am well, Thank you and I have some good news for you. Judge Jackson has vacated the second motion and therefore should be scheduling you for an "Evidentiary hearing" soon. I immediately screamed out "Praise the Lord, Thank you Jesus," I said this is in my favor again? She said "yes," it is, but we may still have a long way to go, because they still can drag this thing out.

I said, I know, because I've been reading lots of cases, and some have taken anywhere from months to years to be decided on. She said that, is true, so I don't want you to get your hopes up too high yet. I said, "I know, I must continue to remain patient."

But, this would be my *fifth miracle happening in the Courthouse. You see, we don't know what's going on behind the scenes. While we're standing in faith, God is over here working on these people and then over there working on those people. He has to work out both of those situations before his plans can come together. We have to rest in peace and confidence, and in communing with him.

You see how "God" used his vessels to get me back into Court.

On May 19, 2014, I received the next motions filed from my Attorney and the government, of course, they were still opposing against me receiving any relief from prison. The enemy wasn't throwing in the towel without a fight yet. But, I will continue to trust in God to judge my case for me, because it's not over until he says it's over. The great news is that the righteous will never be forsaken and given over to their enemies, as all men will be forced by the final judgment to see that there is a God. God, the supreme judge will always judge rightly.

Like David, he was crying out to God and God heard his cry and mines too. Hallelujah and Thank you Jesus!

After what seemed like another long, intense wait, the next communication I heard from the courts via my Attorney was on July 3, 2014. I couldn't understand what was taking them so long to set me up, just a court date. I'm sure you all can relate to how it must feel, when the mind starts to wandering off, to a thousand places.

So for the entire month of "June and July," on every Monday, I fasted on the behalf of my Appeal being won. My evidentiary hearing was set for

September 22-24. I was also told that I'd been assigned a new prosecutor for the motion only.

My Attorney went on to say that he is a former colleague of hers and is very nice, but he does not believe that his supervisors will have any interest in making a new plea offer, to settle the motion, but we would talk about all this in person once we meet. ("You may not even want a new plea offer"), she added. Now at this point, she was starting to confuse me, when she continued on to say, but the bottom line, - I think we are unlikely to get one, unless the Court of Appeals sends your case back for a new trial and that (even if it happens) would be a long way off.

After reading all of this, all I could sense from her, was words of defeat, negative talk and no faith in the accomplishments she had already achieved for me. I almost gave into fear, but I started meditating on all of God's promises on deliverance and faith in asking, until the picture become so clear on the inside of me, nothing could jar it out of me, because it doesn't matter what the government says they are going to do, it's what God says he's going to do in his promises that count and he has me covered already when he said in 1 Peter 3:14 – Do not be afraid of their threats, nor be troubled.

    I couldn't figure out for the life of me, why my Attorney kept stressing how nice this new prosecutor was, when he even told her, that he would be putting up a fight. He did say, however, that he couldn't believe how quickly my motion was moving (maybe for them, but not quickly enough for me, when at this point, I've already been down for five-and-a-half years). He thought that my trial Judge was feeling pressure from the Court of Appeals to deal with the motion. Indeed, he said that in most cases, the judges are inclined to take years to resolve 23-110 motions. So she was very pleased with our progress.

    On the other hand, my trial Judge wasn't so terribly friendly. I started praying after reading this that "God" would go into the robe of this Judge and touch his heart, to a man willing to bless me to a second chance of freedom. I also prayed that he would vacate my sentence and judgment. I continued praying, quoting scriptures again according to "God's" favor on deliverance. Prayer is always the first place to start. It just makes so much sense, because there is power in prayer. Additionally, Proverbs 21:1 clearly emphasizes that, the king's heart is in the hands of the Lord.

Psalm 23:5 – Thou prepares a table for me in the presence of my enemies

CHAPTER 13
THE HEARING

On August 5, 2014, I was called over to R&D to be processed out of Hazelton and transferred back to CCA in Washington, D.C. It was five of us ladies that day going on WRITS. After all shackled up and lead through the last door leading out of the prison, other inmates were yelling at us across the fence. But I recalled, "Cee-Cee" telling me clearly, "don't look back," because you're not coming back and remember the story of "Lot," when God told him not to look back.

The transportation officers drove us about two hours to the air-lift in Pennsylvania to be flown to the "Oklahoma transit center." This would be my first experience flying on an airplane, fully shackled down, but I did not have an ounce of fear in me, in fact I was quite the opposite. I was full of joy and excitement, after having been caged inside of "Hazelton" for four years, who wouldn't been? Once, in Oklahoma, I was detained there for about a week, then back on the plane again headed back to the same destination point in PA. Then the Marshals drove several of us, to this "Andy Griffin" county jail in Warsaw, VA. Luckily, I stayed there just over night. The Marshals picked me up the very next morning and finally I was off to DC. I arrived there on August 12, 2014. It was not a good week for me to arrive there, because the jail was on lock-down for an entire week, while they under- went their contraband shakedown. So after being processed in, I was taken to the lock-down unit. On this unit I would be classified the following week, after everything was over.

    On that Monday, before being classified, the officer informed me that I had a social visit. I kept asking her, twice, was she for sure that she had the right "Jones." She told me that she would call downstairs and verify. The problem was with me, I hadn't been able to put in a visiting slip, because I had been on lock for the entire week, since I was brought in. After, the officer's verification, sure enough the visit was for me. I had not a clue, who was coming to see me, but I would soon find out. Once in the visiting room, to my surprise, it was my brother, "Tyrone," both my daughters, and all of the grand kids. Talk about a wonderful welcome back to DC surprise it was. After the visit, I was returned back to the unit, where I later learned, the reason why I was allowed a visit, was because everything was still in the system, from four years ago, when I left, as it remains in the system for five years.

    I thought it was ironic how "God," knew that I would be back in time, before that expiration date. Once, I was settled into my assigned unit, after being classified, it would be a month-and-a-half, before my evidentiary hearing would be heard, which was September 22-24. After being on the unit for a couple of days, this nice woman, named

Ms. Miles, introduced herself to me. Obviously wanting to be nosey also, she asked me my name and why I was there. Since I've become accustomed to women asking me this question over the years, I didn't mind. One reason was because I'd stopped being ashamed of what I'd done and (2) everyone knows someone who's been a victim of domestic violence, including maybe even their own self.

After answering the question, her response was surprising, "you've been a victim of circumstances," and beginning September 1st, me and you are going to start a prayer circle, each night, up until the night, before you go to court, and pray you out of here, because you are going home! I had to fight back the tears, from falling from my eyes. During the entire time, I had been down, not one inmate had ever offered to pray with me to this extent. My only fear from her, was wondering whether or not, she was actually going to live up to this commitment. Sadly, to say, most of the women

I did time with, their word didn't amount to anything.

I am happy to share with you that Mrs. Miles, remained true to her commitment. We both prayed, every single night, leading up to the night before I would return back to court. During that time, a few more women joined in with us also. We each rotated around, each night taking turns, leading the prayer circle, because the others were also praying for a favorable outcome on their upcoming court cases as well. Until this prayer circle began, I'd never prayed boldly and fervently in front of others. Somehow, I sensed then that "God" was preparing to use me as one of his servants, one day for something.

The hearing day finally arrived. Once, the Marshals lead me upstairs to the courtroom where I would appear in front of Judge Jackson again. While waiting behind the Judge's chamber, I got down on my knees praying to the Father, and standing on the Word, not caring who was watching me on camera, as I am sure someone was.

I quoted many scriptures, because "no scripture, no power," and it glorifies "God" when we abide in his Word and his Word abides in us also. We can ask him for anything, no matter how big the petition, and he will grant us our hearts desire. I ended my prayer with saying Jehovah Nissi, I go into this courtroom victoriously, because I know that no weapon formed against me, is going to prosper.

Once inside the courtroom, upon entering, the Judge greeted all parties, including me. I greeted him back "Good afternoon." Hello, after the preliminaries matters were put out there, my trial attorney, Mr. McCants would be called as the first witness. This would be my first time, laying eyes on him, since I was sentenced. I am reminded by what scripture tells us in Psalms 23:5, I will prepare a table for you, in the presence of your enemies.

After being sworn in, my attorney would be questioning him first on direct examination. The questions asked of him consisted of where did he obtain his law degree, what research services does he use when doing his legal research, did he consult the CPI Manual? Not really, he was aware of them, but not really. When asked next, how much he was paid for my representation, he couldn't remember, but he thought it to be like $19,000. My attorney asked him, was it more like $30,000. No, it wasn't that much money. "You're saying it was $19,000? Yeah. Right there, he had lied, because I'd paid him $28,000. He couldn't even remember my sister's name, that paid him all the money, when asked that question. He did recognize her in the courtroom. He was asked did he take continuing legal education programs. It depended on if any classes would be of interest to him, but basically "no." He couldn't particularly remember exactly what research he conducted or the method, he conducted on behalf of myself.

The next biggest question asked of him, was specifically about one issue of law and whether he researched it and his knowledge just as he went to trial with me and throughout the trial? Did he know the status of the law with respect to the admissibility of a decedent's violent history? He believed so, was his response, and he remembered the issue coming up in trial and he did know that it wasn't his strategy to get in every conviction that "Kerry" had, because he thought what we had was explosive enough.

His strategy also was that the jury got to know me and what I was thinking that night. Next, he wasn't hung up on totally trying to dirty him up. He felt it was plenty out there that would go in front of the jury as far as him trying to run down a person in the wheelchair and some of the other things that he had done. Q. What research into his prior violent history, did you do in order to corroborate my testimony? A. There were three investigators who he had assigned to my case and he named each one of them. Q. Have you reviewed the transcript of this trial? A. Yes. Q. Can you point to a place anywhere in this transcript where you argued that violent criminal history of which she was unaware was admissible? A. Okay, well, no, I can't argue that. I didn't see that in the transcript. I didn't argue that. He also said he was going off what he thought he had learned in law school.

So there it came out, he hadn't researched the law. He didn't know that the law says prior violent history of decedent is admissible, irrespective of the defendant's knowledge. He didn't think it mattered. There were some questions Mr. McCants even became arrogant about when asked by my Attorney. Then she'll say to him, well, if I can frame the question more clearly for you. At another time, he said to her excuse me, then, okay, I'll calm down.

He couldn't recall the exact circumstances to certain events. He was like, you're asking me about something four years ago. He also admitted he didn't intend to introduce anything I didn't know about. He didn't think it was necessary, because there was so much on him, and the stuff was so explosive. He agreed that if he'd told the juror about him shooting a relative, that would've been explosive to put before the jurors. He concluded that he didn't do a perfect trial, but he did try his best to get me back home. In my heart, I respected him for admitting the truth on that. Series of more questions were asked of him on direct, but to make a long story short, once all the exhibits were received into evidence, Court was adjourned for the 22nd.

On the following day the 23rd, I returned back to Court again, for round two. Just as I had done yesterday, I got back down on my knees again, behind the Judge's chamber, praying some more. You can't be ashamed, when you're calling on the Lord, no matter where you are or he'll be ashamed of you. Fight all of your battles, when you drop to your knees, and you win every time.

Once inside the courtroom, the proceedings resumed. Mr. McCants would concede that he didn't know the law as to that particular area, which was the homicide exception for the introduction of past violent acts by the decedent. Since this was clearly established, the government told the Court that they weren't going to do much with him on cross examination today, and were satisfied with the Court making their finding. Therefore, they would be able to wrap things up today, instead of going into another day on the 24th. I was happy to hear that, as I was certainly ready to get this over with and behind me.

    The only issue now before the Court was whether his performance created a sufficient prejudice to the defendant, although the government saw that he didn't know the law, they were still not changing their position from their opposition, in all their motion briefs. Mr. McCants was once again brought unto the witness stand to be cross-examined. It became very confusing to not only myself, but to the Court, my attorney and the government as well, while listening to his testimony. Sometimes, I didn't know whether he was trying to save me from the grave in which he had me buried or continue to throw me up under the bus. In which, at that point, I'll be talking under my breath to the Lord, "No weapon formed against me, shall prosper, then I'll be singing to myself, under my breath as well, there is power in the name of Jesus, to break every chain. Finally, he was released from his testimony and allowed to step down. I couldn't have been more relieved, not to have to continue looking at him.

Shortly afterwards, the hearing was finished. I waited in anticipation, thinking that now the Judge would be ready to make his ruling. I was on pins and needles, heart pounding and everything. Instead of a verdict, the Judge conveyed to both my Attorney and the government that he would give both sides until December 21st to draw up their arguments and present back to him. I'm sitting there saying to myself, in my mind, no he didn't just say that! Who couldn't have been more disappointed was me, because once I returned back to "CCA," everyone would be asking what happened? We'd all claimed that I would be going home, after the hearing. Instead, I would be detained at "CCA" a bit longer, while waiting in limbo and on the Lord.

Surprisingly, I didn't go home then, me and the ladies continued our prayer circle, every single night, each eagerly looking forward to it. I kept on going to Wednesday night Bible studies and services on Sunday, expecting my miracle, any day, because without faith, it's impossible to please "God."

On November 21, 2014, I received my copies of the briefs from my Attorney and the government's opposition, again. They were determined not to stop fighting it, and that was fine, because although they were stronger than me, they weren't stronger than "God." Now since both arguments were in, the next thing to do was to wait on Judge Jackson to make his decision on whether he would vacate my sentence and conviction or deny me, stating that no prejudice was shown in my case. In which case, I still wasn't quite out of the ball park, his decision would return to the Appellate Court and they would make the final decision over his head. I wasn't so worried on his decision, because having faith in "God" meant that I understood that the "Lord" is my strength and shield and I trusted in him with all of my heart.

The smallest worry I had and I prayed to "God" about, was that I didn't want to be sent back to "Hazelton," while waiting on the Judge to make his decision. Which he had no set time to do, according to my Attorney. Winter time had approached, and I didn't want to face another cold and bitter winter up in those mountains, having to go outside everywhere there.

But, the government was so press to get me back there that they notified my Attorney, so she could inform me that they would be coming to pick me up any day, this was around December 3rd. She wanted to give me a heads up, so it wouldn't be an instant surprise whatever morning they came. She did ask though, if he could hold off, until after the

Christmas and New Year's holiday, but he couldn't make her any promises, as the Marshals were pressuring him. Although, disappointed, once again, I didn't care anymore, I told everyone, it didn't matter, because as I started to look at it this way, whether I was still here or there, once the Judge's ruling came in and it's in my favor, they're going to have to bring me right back, so it's obvious they like wasting money in transportation costs. I'll just enjoy the free ride, I guess. I did warn the ladies though and a couple of the correctional officers that I should be back by the spring, watch and see, I told them! Fortunately, the Marshals finally came the morning of January 9th; I was so thankful that they did allow me to stay through both holiday occasions still in D.C., which also afforded me a few more extra visits with my family.

Romans 8:28 – And we know that all things work together for good to those who love God, to those who are the called according to his purpose.

CHAPTER 14
DECISION TIME

On February 3, 2015, when I awakened, this morning, I was a little upset, because twice again the Marshals picked up someone else, whom for the second time came after me. It was like they kept skipping over me. I never thought I would be so in a hurry to get back to "Hazelton West VA." Being at that Mayberry style jail somewhere in Warsaw, Virginia, that is contracted by U.S. Marshals, was the worst month of my time served, being there even one day was like punishment before reaching prison, if one never been to prison before. But still I kept trusting and praying to God telling him that you must be holding me back from something or someone, what is it God? Show me! While in the shower that morning this is what I asked him, then I continued to pray to him, saying "Lord" please let Judge Jackson make his decision one day this week, and lastly Lord, please let these 6 years I just reached be time served and sufficient enough for the crime I committed (Amen).

Less than one hour later, the correctional officer paged into the intercom asking for R. Jones (that was my AKA name they had me under) anyway, I rushed over to the box and answered back, saying this is she. He went on to say, I have a message from your Attorney Ms. Kittay. Now you didn't hear it from me, but she said something about your sentence being vacated. What I was hearing literally knocked me off of my feet for a split second, I paused, because to say I was in a great shock, is an understatement, my heart was hammering, then I finally managed to say, oh Thank you, thank you so much for the message. He then said wait a minute now, do you have her phone number. I said "No." He said, you have something to write it down with, I said "no." A lady standing near me said someone get her a pen or pencil to write with. I was so nervous, I could not write it down, and the lady said, here I'll write it down for you, as the correctional officer read it off. I again said, "Thank you so very much." You're welcome, "he said back." The other inmates starting congratulating me, hugging and hi-fiving me.

Excited doesn't even begin to describe what I felt that moment. But, I finally managed to say in front of them all Thank you Jesus! Next, everyone was as anxious as I was for me to hurry up and call my Attorney. A lady showed me how to transfer money onto the phone to make the call, and once I did so, as soon as my Attorney answered the phone, I was like Ms. Kittay, I got your message, is it really true (the ladies in the background all started laughing, how I said that) she says, yes, it is, we won! I said OMG. Thank you Jesus! She said you and Jackie said the same thing, and you're right, thank you Jesus. She then went on to explain to me other significant things I needed to know and what to expect later on. By the way dear hearts, this would be my *6th Miracle happening in the Courthouse and according to Job 5:19…He should deliver thee in six troubles; yes, in seven there shall no evil touch thee.

Talk about a wonderful day in paradise, it turned out to be. I was so ecstatic about the victory Jesus had won for me, no words can describe that feeling. A couple of days later on that Thursday, I and a couple of more ladies were awakened to learn that we were going to be picked up by the Marshals to go to our designated prisons. Once we got to R&D and sat for about an hour, the Marshals came to let us out that "Mayberry" cell one-by-one, as they told each where they were headed to, the other two ladies were going to Hazelton, but as I was the last one out, he said, but you are going back to D.C. I said "yes, Thank you Jesus," with all smiles. I said to the Marshall, as he shackled me up, see yah took so long to come back and pick me up, now I ended up going back home instead. "I won" my appeal! He just smiled at me, and said nothing, but the other two ladies, we said good-bye to one another, and they wished me good luck again.

When I arrived back to CCA, all the ladies were so shocked to see me back so quickly, I had just left a month ago on January 9th. Upon entering the unit, I told them all, "I won, I won my appeal," everyone began hugging and congratulating me as well. I told several ladies, along with a few of the officers and the case manager, I told you, I would be back by the Spring, but even I didn't think it would be this quick. You sure said it, they replied back. It was amazing how "God" even kept my same room open up for me, with the same roommate I had when I left. She said girl, God must have known you were coming back too, because I only had one roommate since you left, and she only stayed one week. We both said "Nobody but God"!

Funny thing back in December sometime, I had prayed to "God" during one of my prayer times that he wouldn't allow me to see the inside of Hazelton ever again. You see how even "God" has a sense of humor. The Lord laughed at me, while I said that, because he knew my day was coming. Secondly, on December 26, 2014, I dreamed and saw Judge Jackson so clearly, telling me that he was going to release me in April, if not March, but he would not be rushed into it, by my Attorney. The reason he had said this was because at the end of her last brief, she asked that he make his decision, sometime in December. The only person I had told about this dream was my roommate, "Andrea," because I had awakened her that particular night talking in my sleep.

Additionally, after having been transferred and brought back to CCA, after a month gone, I and several of the ladies immediately resumed our prayer circle every single night for the next 2 weeks, until my scheduled court date on the 24th of February.

I had assumed that once Judge Jackson had vacated my sentence and conviction, that I would automatically become a free woman, but it doesn't work like that. My attorney had to file a motion on my behalf, requesting my release. This motion provided the new Judge I was assigned to grant me release, pending the final decision the government could pursue, which consisted of either re-trialing me or offering me an acceptable plea offer.

Upon arriving inside the Court house, it was like the Marshals had been waiting for me. There were only three of us ladies scheduled for Court that day, and each of us were picked up from CCA separately, which was unusual. While un-shackling me, two of the lady Marshals said to me, young lady, are you ready to go home? I said, "Yes I am!"

Once escorted into the courtroom, I felt pretty confident that I was going home! But, it didn't happen on this day, because I was assigned a new Judge, he was not provided time to read everything, because his law clerk had been out of the country, so he set another date for two days later on the 26th.

This time, once I was brought back into the Courtroom, I was faced with several of "Kerry's" family being present and waiting to make their victim impact statement. At first the Judge didn't think it was admissible for them to speak at a bond hearing, stating that was something they do at sentencing hearings only. But, the prosecutor went out her way to show the Judge in black and white, where it stated that this could be allowed. He then granted them an allotted time to speak, but only one came forward and spoke. Sadly, she had gone to great lengths to convey a lie, telling the court that I had met him while working as a correctional officer, and I had access to his prison records. She further added that I shouldn't be granted release back into the community to be able to enjoy the rest of my life, when they lost him 6 years ago this month. I whispered to my attorney to tell her of the lie she had just told. She said, it was ok, it wouldn't make a difference in his decision.

Throughout the rest of the hearing for almost four hours, the prosecutor went out her way again to oppose every argument she could possible come up with, in hopes of stopping the Judge from releasing me, quoting their #one line, of course, that I would be a threat to the community.

After hearing each one of her arguments, the Judge then said, do you realize that each one of these arguments were stated in a 2-week trial by the same Judge that has signed off for her sentence and conviction to be vacated. Stating that her prospects for acquittal would have greatly increased had she had effective counsel and you want me to overrule his decision. It is also to my understanding that domestic violence cases have the lowest recidivism rate.

My family, Attorney and I saw the enemy on a war path, so determined to keep me down, but in the end, we also saw "God" at work, in full action.

The enemy was stronger than me, but they weren't stronger than "God". When we heard the Judge say that he was granting me my release, one of Kerry's family members yelled out, that's Bullshit. At that point, they all were escorted out by the Marshals. I, on the other hand, stood there in awe, while thanking Jesus, under my breath. My attorney patted me in the back, as to congratulate me on going home. The government, I can only imagine, felt humiliated at their lost.

My sister Jacqueline was called up to the Judge's bench to be asked a couple of critical questions, then granted my release into her custody. The Judge placed me on a trial period, pending my next Court appearance March 25th, to be on a High intensity ankle bracelet, 24-hour home confinement, with the exceptions of only going outside my sister residence for Court appearance, Attorney visits, and to report once a week to pre-trial services and take urine tests. I was fine with all of this, because these conditions, sure beat walking around in prison any day. Once the Marshals escorted me back downstairs to the cell-block, I must have thanked "God" a thousand times so to speak, mumbling to myself, not caring who was looking at me, I got down on my knees and thanked "God" for my deliverance. You rescued me from the miry pit and didn't let me sink, or the flood waters sweep over me or the deep swallow me up. Thank you Jesus, you have just delivered my soul from death. Thank you so very much for granting me favor even in the sight of my captors. (AMEN). You see, we serve a God who can just step right in and have everyone saying what just happened?

    Several hours later, the Marshals were ready to take us all back to the "CCA" to be processed out and released. I was taken back to my unit at that time to pack up their property and retrieve what little paperwork I had. All the ladies were so very happy for me that I was finally going back home again. We hugged and said our good-byes, and afterward, the escort officer came to pick me up and walk me over to the catwalk, leading to the D.C. Jail, to wait further processing out. Once there, I was given a grey sweat suit and denim jacket to wear out. As it was a cold and frigid night, at almost 9 pm, my daughter, her boyfriend, and their daughter had been waiting hours for me to come out, but they weren't going to leave me (LOL). As the officer opened up the gates for me, on the other side of the fence awaiting was my baby daughter, yelling in excitement, "Ma, Ma," and it was the happiest day for the both of us, as we hugged and cried together. It was at this time that I personally met her baby's father, for the first time and greeted and hugged him too. As my daughter drove off, I still couldn't believe that I was actually in a real car, driving away into the free world again. It was a reality too good to be true. It was a feeling, I will never forget. But, scripture reminds me, according to Jeremiah 29:13-14, I will bring you to the place from which I caused you to be carried away captive.

I'm here to tell you dear hearts, prayer and fasting will get you out of more situations than money can any time. Take me for instance, I paid my defense attorney $28 thousand dollars and what did it get me, a conviction of 20 years. It took the power of prayer to get me out. I'm telling you dear beloved's that if you don't read or listen to the Word of God, you won't have any faith or strength to resist the devil when he starts telling you that you're going to lose the battle. You are going to need all the faith in you to rebuke him in the name of Jesus!

Overall, I stood in faith for 6 years, letting patience do its perfect work, by living according to the Word of God. No matter how impossible your situation looks, you've got to keep your eyes on God and the living Word, not the enemy and you will come out a winner every time. I looked forward to this day for six years, when I would finally take off my prison clothes and be able to serve you with twenty times more determination. Even now, I sing Jeremiah's song of gladness and joy. "O give thanks unto the Lord, for he is good, for his mercy endures forever." Psalms 118:29. Now, thanks be unto God which always causes us to triumph in Christ. 2 Corinthians 2:14.

1 John 4:4 – Ye are of God, little children, and have overcome them: because greater is he that is in you, than he that is in the world

CHAPTER 15
MANKIND vs. GOD

I just happened to call my Attorney on a legal call, asking her to clear up something for me. What did she mean in her recent letter, when she said that Judge Jackson had no dead line to make his decision? "She said," it meant that he could take anywhere from now, until several weeks, months or even years. Then she went on to give me an example even of a case where there was one Judge who sat on this man's motion for years. Well, the man ended up dying while still incarcerated and this Judge then says, oh well, I guess now I don't have to answer to it! She also said that Judge Jackson was terribly unfriendly.

Lastly, she wanted to also tell me that she had just spoken to the U.S. Attorney's office and he had told her that the Marshals were ready to pick me up and send me back to West Virginia, while waiting for the Judge to make his decision, since it was no time frame, and it was because the longer I had remained at the CCA, I was not allotted in their housing budget. She told me also that she asked him, if he could hold off, until she had time to prepare me and also if he could hold off until after Christmas at least. He couldn't make her any guarantees, because the Marshals were pressuring him and she wanted to warn me, so it wouldn't be a surprise the morning they came to pick me up.

    I was hoping to perhaps stay at "CCA" until his decision came in and that I would never have to return back to see the inside of that prison again. That was my prayer. 1 Peter 3:14 tells us do not be afraid of their threats nor be troubled.

    Well, gratefully I felt blessed that the Marshals did omit me, until after Christmas and the New Years' both. I'm sure though, they couldn't wait until I was back in BOP's custody, because they picked me up the morning of January 9, 2015. That's when I was dropped off at that county jail in "Warsaw, VA," and remained there for almost a month, until Judge Jackson's ruling came in, and they had to re-route me back to Washington, DC to the "CCA." You see how God stepped in at the nick of time, because he had the final say. They dug a pit for me ahead of time, but they fell into it instead.

Remember in Chapter 11, when I told you that the first Appeal's Attorney couldn't find any legal grounds, well take a look at that letter for yourself on the next page. Also, refreshing your memory back to Chapter 12, when I told you about what the new prosecutor had said, "he didn't believe that his supervisors would have any interest in making a new plea offer, to settle the motion," and her response was that I may not even want a new plea offer, but the bottom line, I think is that we are unlikely to get one. Now watch this, two weeks after I'd been released from incarceration, the government was offering me a plea offer that consisted of eight years all suspended, minus the time I already served, no additional prison time and three years' probation. My attorney told me that she never knew the government to offer a plea-deal like that in a homicide case. So who's the Boss?

What the government didn't know was God was in control of my destiny, not them and that no weapon formed against me would prosper, because he is the Great I am.

District of Columbia Court of Appeals

No. 10-CF-984

MOZELLA JONES,
    Appellant,

v.

UNITED STATES,
    Appellee.

2009 CF1 2519

FILED SEP 1 1 2012
DISTRICT OF COLUMBIA COURT OF APPEALS

ORDER

On consideration of the motion of court-appointed counsel to withdraw from this appeal pursuant to *Anders v. California*, 386 U.S. 738 (1967), *Gholson v. United States*, 532 A.2d 118 (D.C. 1987); and *Gale v. United States*, 429 A.2d 177 (D.C. 1981), *cert. denied*, 454 U.S. 893 (1981), it is

ORDERED that the appellant shall, no later than **October 3, 2012**, file any response showing, with specificity, any reason why counsel's motion should not be granted and the conviction, order or judgment on appeal affirmed. If you do not respond the court will consider the matter on the motion submitted by counsel and the record on appeal. It is

FURTHER ORDERED that the motion of court-appointed counsel to withdraw is hereby held in abeyance pending appellant's response to this order.

BY THE COURT:

/s/ Eric T. Washington

ERIC T. WASHINGTON
Chief Judge

Copies to:

Rosetta D. Jones a.k.a. Mozella Jones
FR #42635-007
USP HAZELTON
P.O. Box 2000
Bruceton Mills, WV 26525

Thomas D. Engle, Esquire
601 Pennsylvania Ave., NW
Suite 900 South
Washington, DC 20004

lw

District of Columbia
Court of Appeals

FILED
SEP 11 2012
DISTRICT OF COLUMBIA
COURT OF APPEALS

TO: Rosetta D. Jones a.k.a. Mozella Jones
FR #42635-007
USP HAZELTON
P.O. Box 2000
Bruceton Mills, WV 26525

RE: No. 10-CF-984 - *Mozzella Jones v. United States*

    Your court-appointed counsel in case no. **2009 CF1 2519** has filed a motion to withdraw from your appeal. If the court grants the motion it will also affirm your conviction or the order or judgment from which you appealed and your appeal will be over. If you believe that you have meritorious issues that you want this court to address you must file a response to your attorney's motion by the date listed in the attached order. This is your chance to tell the court what you believe the trial court did wrong in handling your case or what you think your trial attorney did or failed to do that hurt your case. The key is to focus on what happened during your trial court proceedings. A self-addressed stamped envelope is provided for you to mail your response.

    The court will consider counsel's motion when the time listed in the order has passed. If you file a timely response opposing the motion, the court will also consider your opposition at that time. The court will also review the record on appeal, including the transcript of the proceedings, and any written motions that your trial counsel filed in Superior Court. If the court concludes that the appeal lacks merit and grants the motion of your court-appointed counsel to withdraw, your conviction or the order or judgment on appeal will be affirmed. Otherwise, the court will take appropriate action, which may include denying your counsel's motion to withdraw from your appeal or appointing new counsel to continue your appeal. Therefore, it is important that you file a response to the motion if you believe there are grounds for appeal.

Sincerely,

Julio A. Castillo

JULIO A. CASTILLO
Clerk of the Court

Copies to:

Thomas D. Engle, Esquire
601 Pennsylvania Ave., NW
Suite 900 South
Washington, DC 20004

lw

Psalm 37:7 – "Rest in the Lord and wait patiently for him"

CHAPTER 16

RESTING IN GOD'S PROMISES

God says if we believe his Word and speak it, then the father within us does the work and brings it to pass, because faith by itself, it does not have works, it is dead (James 2:17) God's will is in his Word.

Ephesians 3:20 – God is able to do exceedingly, abundantly, beyond and above all that we ask for.

Isaiah 54:17 – No weapon formed against me shall prosper.

Isaiah 65:24 – It shall come to pass that before they call, I will answer; and while they are still speaking, I will hear.

Jeremiah 33:3 – Call unto me, and I will answer you, and show you great and mighty things, which thou know not.

1 John 3:22 – We receive whatever we ask of God because we do those things that are pleasing in his sight.

1 John 4:4 – He who is you (Mozella), which is (God) is greater than he who is in the world.

John 11:22 – Whatsoever thou will ask of God, God will give you.

John 14:13 – And whatever you ask in my name that I will do.

John 14:14 – If you ask anything in my name. I will do it!

John 15: 7 – If you remain in me, and my words remain in you, ask for whatever you want and it will be done for you or if you abide in me and my words abide in you, you will ask what you desire and it shall be done for you.

John 16:24 – Until now you have asked nothing in my name. Ask and you will receive, that your joy may be full.

Mark 11:24 – What things so ever you desire, when you pray believe that you receive them and you shall have them.

Mathew 7:7 – Ask and it will be given to you.

Matthew 7:8 – For everyone who asks receives.

Matthew 18:19-20 – If two of you agree on earth concerning anything that they ask, it will be done for them, by my father in heaven (v.20). For where 2 or 3 are gathered together, in my name, I am there in the midst of them.

Matthew 21:22 – Whatever you ask for in prayer with faith, you will receive.

Psalms 34:17 – The righteous cry and the Lord hears and deliver them out of all their troubles.

Psalms 50:15 – Call unto me in the day of trouble; I will deliver you (Mozella) and you shall glorify me.

Psalms 91:14 – Because he has set his love upon me, therefore I will deliver her (Mozella)

Psalms 91:15 – (Mozella) will call upon me, and I will answer her; I will be with her in trouble; I will deliver her and honor her.

I believed in each one of these promises and faithfully meditated on them, because God's will is accomplished when someone is believing for it to be, trusting him with all his heart and leaning not unto his own understanding (Proverbs 3:5). I found this reminder to trust encouraging also – Romans 4:20-21. (Mozella) did not waiver through unbelief being fully convinced that what (God) had promised he was also able to perform. I told God my request, he performed it, because he is all powerful and I thank him for his faithfulness.

Waiting for God's timing may also give us a greater miracle than we had hoped for. Also according to Hebrews 6:11-12 tells us that if we keep God's promises in the soul of your heart, be patient and you will reap the harvest of a wonderful future.

ON SEEKING GOD

"Proverbs 8:35 – For whosoever find me, find life and shall obtain favor of the Lord"

Amos 5:4 – Seek ye me, and ye shall live.

1 Chronicles 16:11 – Seek the Lord and his strength; seek his face evermore.

2 Chronicles 15:2 – The Lord is with you, while ye be with him, and if ye seek him, he will be found of you, but if ye forsake him, he will forsake you.

Deuteronomy 4:29 – Thou shall seek the Lord thy God, thou shall find him, if thou seek him with all thy heart and will all thy soul.

Hebrews 11:6 – For he that cometh to God must believe that he is, and that he is a rewarder of them that diligently seek him.

Hosea 10:12 – For it is time to seek the Lord, until he come and rain righteousness upon you.

Isaiah 55:6-7 – Seek the Lord while he may be found, call upon him while he is near. Let the wicked forsake his way, and the unrighteous man his thoughts.

Jeremiah 29:13 – And ye shall seek me, and find me, when ye shall search for me with all your heart.

Lamentations 3:25 – The Lord is good unto them that wait for him; to the soul that seeketh him.

Matthews 6:33 – Seek ye first the kingdom of God and his righteousness and all these things shall be added unto you.   Once you seek God with all your heart and soul, he will open up so many doors of blessings for you.

Matthew 7:7-8 – Ask, and it will be given to you; seek, and you will find; knock, and it will be opened to you. For everyone who asks receives, and he who seeks finds, and to him who knocks it will be opened.

Proverbs 8:17 – I love those who love me, and those who seek me diligently will find me.

Psalms 119-10 - With my whole heart, I have sought you; oh, let me not wander from your commandments.

Psalms 34:10 – But they that seek the Lord shall not want any good thing.

John 20:27 – "Jesus said stop doubting and believe"

CHAPTER 17
AMAZING GRACE (MY CHAINS ARE GONE)

It's not going to happen, "Satan kept trying to convince me. You might as well erase that thought from your mind." "I know it's unlikely, I said, but it's not impossible! So I declare "Satan," you are a liar, if the truth ain't in you, and I rebuke you, in the name of Jesus! So you might as well take your hands off of my appeal.

God makes impossible things happen, because I hear stories all the time, and I've read volumes of case laws, while in prison. The Bible tells us in Ephesians 3:20-21, Now to him who is able to do immeasurably more than all we ask or imagine, according to his power that is at work within us, to him be glory in the church and in Christ Jesus throughout all generations, forever and ever! Amen.

This was the year (2015) that God chose to do "immeasurably more" in my family. He replaced indifference with love. How did he do it? Beats me! But I saw it happen, and why should I be surprised? If Satan can turn love into indifference, certainly God can change indifference back into love.

"Prayer"

Lord, Thank you for doing immeasurably more in my life, than I could ever have imagined. I am so thankful that you are able and often do make impossible situations possible.

The old adage is true. "Timing is everything"! That's why Paul's statement, "when the fullness of the time had come, God sent forth his son." Intrigues me so much (Galatians 4:4)

God's timing is perfect in everything. While you are waiting, perhaps wondering why God doesn't seem to be acting on your behalf, remember that he's working behind the scenes to prepare his moment of intervention at just the right time. Trust him, he knows what time it is.

God will do what seems impossible! Just when we think there is no way out of our mess, God will prove to us how strong and wonderful he is on our behalf **(see Chronicles 16:9).**

I am convinced it was because of praying Psalm 91 every day, intercessory prayer and fasting monthly, that God delivered me on my appeal. God was faithful, I believed, I trusted and God set a captive free like me. God said in Psalm 86:7, In your day of trouble, I will call upon thee, for thou will answer me. I would pray "Lord," I am calling on you to help get me outta this jam, I put myself into, and he heard my petition and came to my rescue. I was in a precarious position but God didn't leave me there.

Let the redeemed of the Lord tell their story; whom he hath redeemed from the hand of the enemy. Psalm 107:2.

I am a living testimony to God's faithfulness to his promises. I kept abiding in God's Word and trusting him to be faithful. God's hand was in my life the entire time.

I don't know how I made it through, but I sit back and I count my blessings. I have felt the pain and confinement of shackles and tribulation. Satan wanted me, he wasn't fooling around. He wanted to "take me out" and sift me in the wind. It is frightening to think how close he came to doing it! But, "God" who is rich in mercy, saved me.

My closest friends had given up on me, it was over pretty much before I had even gotten sentenced, then "Jesus" prayed too and called me out of the tomb, just like he did with "Lazarus," so I could sit at his table. I have been through hell, but I made it out. I faced a crushing challenge, but I survived, by his grace, and I am a living miracle. Every time anyone sees me, my life shouts out, "God is real." The enemy wanted to terminate my joy, peace, and prosperity, but he failed. I want to shout to the world, I made it, and who woke me up out of my sleep and unraveled my problems - Nobody but "Jesus." I endured extreme attacks from the media to pay the price for the harvest, now it's time to reap the rewards!

Mozella, didn't let a hurtful past or an unpromising present, keep her from asking God for a huge blessing. God had a plan to help me get out and reach across boundary lines and touch lives for him. I trusted the Lord that he knows what he's doing in his perfect plan laid out for my life.

I knew that I had gotten way over my head, and now that I was in it, all I could do was continue to sink or swim, I chose to "swim." Thankfully, I had God's hand upon me. I was able to get through this experience successfully and I saw his hand at work every step of the way. He took an ordinary person like me and turned me into the extraordinary. Praise God!! Astounding!!

On February 26, 2015, I was released from prison. As I walked through the jail gates, I had many thoughts. Previously, I doubted that I would ever be released this soon. I had seen so many women that had been down for 15, 20, 25 years for the same charge I had. God was good to me, and I was sure, in my mind, that I wasn't ever going to disappoint him again.

I went through a horrible time, on that fatal night, but Jesus interceded on my behalf. Justice demanded that I stay in prison until 2026, but mercy threw the case out of court. Jesus however knew the power of a second chance. He forgives, heals and restores.

The Lord had brought me out of a prison, even as he did Peter, Act 12:17. God has blessed me all that I lost through sin. The Lord could have saved me and left me in prison, but he brought me out for his glory!

"I was in prison and ye came unto me." Psalms 146:7, "The Lord sets the prisoners free."

It doesn't matter what the circumstances in your life are, if you will only praise the Lord and give him thanks, you will see him do great wonders for you. He is a fair and just God, and he will work mighty on your behalf, if only you will trust in him and praise him for what he is doing in your life.

I am going to reiterate: The enemy (government) didn't expect me to come out of my situation, because I was so dumbfounded to the law and careless on the scene. "Yes," I lacked skills in both, but what they didn't know was how faithful I was in abiding in God's Word in intercessory prayer, praise and worship. They thought that I was already defeated and that the victory would be won by them instead.

The enemy wasn't expecting anybody to be covering me and praying for me and the heavenly hosts backing me up. In other words, the presence of God was going to shine in my situation, until I was completely delivered. "God" says "you aren't going to die in this mess." I'm going to hold back the sun, because in order to fight you have to be able to see. When the enemy kills you in the dark, I'm going to let the light of my Word begin to shine in your spirit until you are completely delivered.

There were many of days when I felt so discouraged, depressed and feeling like "man," I done messed up. There was somebody else that was fighting for me. The Lord was fighting for me; he did not fail me, although I failed myself. He came through for me in the biggest way, I never would've imagined, but I had a responsibility too!

There was a triple fight going on. I was fighting, my family and friends was fighting for me and the Word was fighting for me. I was being delivered by the Word. "Martin Luther King Jr." couldn't have said it any better for me. "Thank God" almighty I am free-at-last!!!

Praise the Lord Jesus and to God be the Glory, my chains are gone…

I recall from one of T.D. Jakes book, him quoting this, my sister you have something to give to life, in your senior years. Your latter days will be glorious. God will restore what you have lost. Just like he did with "Naomi," from the Bible, she was about to give up hope, but she was wrong, her best days were ahead of her and she didn't even know it. Naomi's latter years were greater than her former ones. She knew a kind of joy in her old age that she hadn't known in her youth. God was on her side, just as he will be with me.

Lord knows, I was facing a big Goliath, like David thought he was. My case was a huge one, and I knew that God had his work cut out on it, but it wasn't too big for him after all. He knew how to get around the enemy, because he laughed at the impossibilities and cried out, it shall be done (Mozella). The Lord delivered me, because it was his desire and he did so in a way, even I didn't expect. In spite of our mistakes, God gives second chances. Look at me! I'm living proof.

His Word promises also they that sow in tears shall reap in joy; he that go forth and weep, bearing precious seed, shall doubtless come again with rejoicing, bringing his sheaves with him. Psalm 126:5-6.

Proverbs 8:35 – "For who so findeth me, findeth life and shall obtain favor of the Lord."

CHAPTER 18
STARTING OVER

I have been blessed going in and blessed going out. A season ends, a season begins. "Yes," God truly blessed me immeasurably more than I could have asked, thought or imagined. Deuteronomy 28:3, 6, 8.

I can hear God's still voice speaking to me and saying - I love you, "Mozella." Don't be afraid. Walk on through. I'm here with you and I'm already there with you. Remember that as long as there is breath, there is hope.

So cast all of your cares, anxieties and frustrations on him. He didn't resurrect you to rebury you under the old worries and stresses. No one can appreciate new beginnings as well as a person, who really needs one!

I can't wait to smell the freshness of the morning and rejoice that I somehow survived. This is my day. There were some who never expected me to make it, but I am here. "If no one makes you a cake, throw your own party!" I sure am.... "Celebrate what God has done for you!"

"I sure am," and recline in the presence of the Lord, in the cool of evening, when the birds softly sing and the day closes like a curtain, he has not failed me, he has held all my weight, so lie back on him. I learned from "Lazarus." Rest in God's presence.

I'm sure my enemies weren't glad I survived, but I'm not moved by that, because I know that "God" is able. Once you develop the tenacity to survive, you are ready to do great things for God. You become unstoppable. Resurrection changes the way you react to fear and death. It doesn't mean you will never fear again. It simply means you will forever react to fear differently. Survival breeds confidence.

No one can threaten me with death again. I have already been dead. Like an ex-convict -- I declare that I have served my time! Release me quickly and let me go. I am free again….

You will only understand what I mean by "survival mode," after you have been crushed and locked in prison, left to die, or forsaken by others. Once you know that you have survived, you could "dig your way out of east hell with a plastic spoon," as long as "God" was with you."

I'm going to maximize this moment. Not enough time to tell you how he saved my soul and set me free and made me whole. He's been so good to me. The devil knocked me down, but "Jesus," raised me up again.

I never preached a message like Lazarus. I'm better than a sermon in words, my life is a sermon in action! I am a walking sermon.

The naysayers were so sure they had the last word, that when they saw a higher power reverse the decision and pull life out of death, I'm sure they were amazed and astonished. The enemy didn't want to surrender me without a fight.

All I can say is that, if I hadn't gone through what I went through, I wouldn't have known "God's" miracles to be real. The Lord saw how I was wronged and he judged my case. (Lamentations 3:59)

Oh how, I love the name "Jesus." Something about the name "Jesus," it is the sweetest name I know… It's sweeter than honey, and can't nobody do what he does, there's power in that name.

There were times, I felt like I was holding on for dear life, but God came through for me. I would say to myself, he didn't rescue me from the river to see me drown in the sea. Oh, but I'm here to share with you that God heard my cry and came to my rescue. "To God be the Glory!"

Remember, the story of Lot's wife, "Don't look back," they'll be a time in your life, when you can glance on it.

I cannot do anything about what I have done in the past, but I can do something about my new future. I am going to enjoy my life and have what Jesus died for me to have. I am going to let go of the past and go on pursuing God from this day fourth. I know that it will take some courage to let go the past, but a strong Christian receives the fullness of God's blessings.

Once we have experience the favor of God, we must never go back. The God of Abraham, Isaac and Jacob is the God of provision.

Praying my way out of prison was the biggest, boldness, fervent and effectual prayers I'd ever prayed to God, in my life. I kept on asking over and over again, just like in Matthew 7:7, tells us to do so. Then, Ephesians 3:20, tells us God is able to do exceedingly, abundantly, beyond and above all that we ask for. God was faithful in his promises.

What was my secret? I put the Word of God first place in my life. I meditated on it, believed it and obeyed it.

"Mozella," my child, your cries have been heard in heaven. Your prayers have been answered. I thank God, I can say with conviction, that what others intended for my harm, God used for my good.

My answered prayers were simply the consequences of abiding in "Jesus." As I walk out of these doors, I'll be celebrating the new woman who God has created me to be. I'll be the same person, the circumstances just changed, but I didn't. We might as well own up to our wrongs, because we can't hide them from God anyway.

My case looking from the supernatural seemed hopeless, but with God on your side, "Thank God," there are no hopeless cases. Likewise, when we make a mistake in life, we can always ask God for forgiveness and start over again, because the Lord says "forget the former things, do not dwell on the past." (Isiah 43:18), so God doesn't have to tell me twice, I'm going to follow his leading, and press toward the mark for the prize of the high calling of God in Christ Jesus. That's my motto now.

I don't know what will come this day or further into the future, but I'm grateful that God will be by my side, and I'll be praying that he grants me with a spirit of praise and thanksgiving in whatever lies ahead, for my future calling.

But, I do know this, I have trusted in your faithful love; right now my heart is rejoicing in your deliverance. For you shall go out with joy and be lead forth with peace (Isaiah 55:12).

I was blessed to achieve a great measure of success, even while in prison. I stepped out on faith and on the Word. The only thing I understand, was that I was set up to be blessed, as a result, I have weathered some storms and endured some controversy, as you can probably imagine how people talked about me, due to this ordeal, but we live in a society that values free speech, so people can say anything they want to about me or about you. Our job is to live in such a way that we validate what is true and render the untruths utterly preposterous.

I am living proof indeed that if you hold on and do not give up, you can survive imprisonment. I have accepted this ordeal of my life as one grand learning experience, realizing that education is all around you. If I'd done anything in life worth attention, this was definitely it.

Isaiah 54:17 – "No weapon formed against me shall prosper:"

CHAPTER 19
ANGEL IN THE COURTROOM

I want to thank you from the bottom of my heart for having gotten this far, reading my book. You may perhaps be curious though as to why I've choose this title, and I'd like to share with you why?

You see after I went to trial, lost and was sentenced, I had pretty much thrown in the towel. I thought it was over for me, because I'd been defeated by the enemy, but little did I realize, it wasn't over until "God" said so, because as we know, he is the "Alpha and the Omega," the beginning and the end; First and the Last.

When things started turning around for me, it all started from in the very same courthouse that I was convicted and sentenced in. The odds for me winning were pretty slim-to-zero," so I thought.

In Acts 12:1-6 describes a situation in which Peter's odds of survival were very low. He was in prison, bound with two chains between two soldiers while others guarded the door (v.6). Herod had already executed one of Jesus' closest followers, and he had the same fate in mind for Peter (vv.1-3). A gambler would not have put any money on Peter getting out of this alive (v.11) And when Peter had come to himself, he said, "Now I know for certain that the Lord has sent his angel and has delivered me from the hand of (the government). As he did with me also.

Yet God's plan for Peter included a miraculous deliverance that even those who were interceding for him found it hard to believe (vv.13-16). They were astonished when he showed up at their prayer meeting.

God can operate outside the odds, because he is all powerful. Nothing is too hard for him. The one who loves us and gave himself for us is in charge of our lives. In ordinary circumstances and impossible situations, God can reveal his power. Whether we are showered with success or sustained in sorrow, he is with us. Jesus said in Matthew 14:26 – It's impossible for human beings, but **all** things are possible for God.

God is always in control behind the scenes. I know that intercessory prayer works for me and for others. Things happen that simply cannot be explained by coincident or accident or fantasy or illusion or any known law for that reason or predictability. Again, the proof is in the experiences, and no one will admit more quickly than I, that until you've had the experience, it is hard to believe.

I have much to learn and a long way to grow. But, I have discovered that the Holy Spirit can do things in loving ways through me, for me, and for others, that I can't do for myself. He can plan events beyond my imagination and carry out projects beyond my strength. I've found that spectacular and unbelievable results occur when I pray as if my life depends on it, as of course, it did.

God gave me my life back. He blessed me with a second chance, more than I deserved. Psalms 103:10 tells us that, he has not dealt with us according to our sins, nor punished us according to our iniquities. If God never does anything more than just redeem me, he has already done enough and far more than I deserved. Like the psalmist says "as the heavens are high above the earth, so great is his mercy toward those who fear him. When God calls, God equips, and he offers to let us start over again, when we make mistakes.

And, that about wraps it up. God is strong and he wants you strong (Mozella). So take everything the master has set out for you, well-made weapons of the best materials. And put them to use so you will be able to stand up to everything the Devil throws your way, in the future.

So you see folks, we can't go wrong, waiting and trusting in the Lord. We have all been victims of unfairness and some of us have weathered inhumane or even criminal treatment as well. It's soul crushing, to be sure and yet we must proactively pick ourselves up, take back control and make a plan that works for restoring our health and peace of mind.

God's Favor

Remember this truth always, you are a child of the King and the promises of his Word are for you. Believe fully in God's favor, learn to trust in it, have the faith to ask for it and finally, learn to act on it and you will live in his favor forever more.

Exodus 3:21 – Favor restores everything the enemy has stolen.

2 Chronicles 20:15-30 – Favor secures great victory in the midst of daunting odds.

Esther 5:8 – Favor grants petition even by ungodly authorities.

Esther 8:5-8 – Favor changes policies, rules, regulations and laws on our behalf.

Psalms 5:11-12 – Favor provides a protective shield over our life.

Psalms 37:5 – Favor lasts for a lifetime and it gives us confidence.

Proverbs 8:35 – For whoso findeth me findeth life and shall obtain favor of the Lord.

Psalms 147:1 – Praise the L*ORD*!
For it is good to sing praises to our God;
For it is pleasant, and praise is beautiful.

CHAPTER 20
SONGS THAT GOT ME THROUGH

One of my favorite songs was written by Bill and Gloria Gaither. This song has given me much inspiration during difficult times. The chorus says, "Because he lives, I can face tomorrow." Because he lives, all fear is gone. Because I know he holds the future and life is worth the living, just because he lives.

Whenever, I felt discouraged and having a bad day, I'd put on all of my praise songs, to keep me perked up and encouraged in the Lord. I wanted to share a few of them with you all, in which I've listed next.

Whatever fire you are going through, keep on singing the praises of God. Keep declaring,

"Because he lives, I can face tomorrow." Because he lives, all fear is gone. And God will deliver you. Just, as he delivered Peter, David, Paul and me….

"Songs," that got me through

1. He has his hands on you (Marvin Sapp)
2. I never lost my Praise (The Brooklyn Tabernacle Choir)
3. I Believe (Marvin Sapp)
4. Clean up (The Canton Spirituals)
5. You're next in line for a miracle (Shirley Caesar)
6. Blessing in the Storm (Kirk Franklin & Family)
7. Turning Around for me (Vashawn Mitchell)
8. "Yes" (Shekinah Glory)
9. I told the Storm (Greg O'Quin N' Joyful Noize)
10. He's Done enough (Beverly Crawford)
11. Let Go (Dewayne Woods)
12. I'm Gonna be Ready (Yolanda Adams)
13. I don't mind waiting (Jonathan Butler & Juanita Bynum)

14. No Weapon (Fred Hammond & Radical for Christ)
15. My time for God's favor (Kurt Carr)
16. Breakthru (Greg O'Quin & Praise)
17. We Fall Down (Donnie McClurkin)
18. God favored me Part I & II (Hezekiah Walker)
19. Not the time, Not the Place (Marvin Sapp)
20. It's been worth having the Lord in my life (Shirley Caesar)
21. The Battle is the Lord's (Yolanda Adams)
22. Through the Storm (Yolanda Adams)
23. The Master Plan (Tamela Mann)
24. I smile (Kirk Franklin)
25. My testimony (Marvin Sapp)
26. Never would have made it (Marvin Sapp)
27. Amazing Grace (My chains are gone)
28. Sinner's Prayer (Detrick Haddon)
29. Ooh wee another blessing (Melvin Williams)
30. All things are working (Fred Hammond)

31. Give Thanks (Marvin Sapp)
32. Lord send your anointing (Marvin Sapp)
33. Still I Rise (Yolanda Adams)
34. My Blessing is on the Way (Alvin Darling)
35. No chains on me (Chris Tomlin)
36. I have decided to follow Jesus (Maratha Promise Band)
37. I've got a testimony (Rev. Clay Evans)
38. He's on Time (Derrick Starks & Today's Generation)
39. Second Chance (Hezekiah Walker & the Love Fellowship Crusade Choir)
40. When you've been Blessed (Patti Labelle)
41. Without You (Maurette Clark)
42. The storm is over now (God's Property)
43. Holy Spirit Rain Down (Alvin Slaughter)
44. Break Every Chain (Tasha Cobbs)
45. Miracle (The Clark Sisters)
46. Bounce Back from your set Back (The Gospel Miracles)

47. Hold Out (The Gospel Miracles)
48. I found Jesus--take a look at me (The Enchoaires)
49. Lord you brought me through (The Enchoaires)
50. It's Working (William Murphy)

Another one of my favorite songs and the best hymns of all time, probably yours too, is "Amazing Grace" by John Newton. Lives rooted in God's unchanging grace can never be uprooted.

> Amazing grace how sweet the sound
> That saved a wretch like me!
> I once was lost but now am found
> Was blind but now I see.

For by grace you have been saved through faith (Ephesians 2:8). The pages of the Bible resonate with music. The Psalms, often called "the Bible Songbook," point us to the love and faithfulness of God. They conclude with an unending call to worship. Let everything that has breath praise the Lord, Praise the Lord (Psalm 150:6).

Today, we need God's ministry of music in our hearts as much as any time in history. Whatever each day brings, may the evening find us singing praise and worship songs to our Lord God.

CHAPTER 21
POEMS

That's Life!!!

Though this sounds cliché that's life, the rage and hurt and frustration that I'm feeling, I know I need to let it out, and let it be behind me, so I can move on, I keep telling myself, I will heal as time goes by, and that I shouldn't put too much into what people are saying about me or what they think of me now, that I'm sitting in a Federal prison, because "that's life," because it's been planted in our minds that success is measured by the terms of others, what they think or how they see us and that's normal, but we put too much into that. It's actually gotten out of control because it has made many to suffer low self-esteem and depression. People have lost their minds worrying from anxiety and stresses of life, but "that's life" …. but when we fall short and we rise up, if we are wise, we can and try real hard to keep matters straight.

How do we avoid letting life's negative get to us? Acknowledge the hurt, go thru a grieving process and then parlay the event into something better. Resilient women learn the lesson and move on.

What are the common obstacles we let get in Joy's way? We have got to stop looking for answers outside of ourselves. Even if you have been wronged, ask yourself if you are going to stay being a victim or figure out how to move to higher ground and be victorious.

"Remember when"

"I remember" when not very long ago, I had my freedom, I wasn't confided to nobody's prison. "I remember," when I use to get up in the mornings to go to a real 9-5 job that paid me a nice salary. "I remember" when I was raising 2 daughters and a grandson and how special that was to me, I had obligations like cleaning up an entire house, cooking meals and paying bills, shopping and traveling on vacations. "I remember" when I loved life, just period, and in general.

"Love yourself first and everything else falls into line." Lucille Ball

I know that when I choose to love myself first everything else will fall into line, because others around me will see that light shining inside me, without me having to say a word. If you love yourself people will know by the way you carry yourself, the way you dress, fix your hair and treat yourself all together, but if they see you don't give a damn about any of these characteristics, then neither will they, but most important just be yourself and everything else will fall into line.

The tongue of a man is his sword
The Husia, translated by Dr. Maulana Karenga

Wars do not begin when one force is aggressive toward another. They begin when one force speaks aggression toward another. No act of aggression begins without a word. The word ignites the warrior mechanism in the mind and body. When we hear aggressive words, we are compelled to respond. When we speak aggressive words, we are advanced upon. A wise soldier knows never to draw his sword unless he is ready, able and willing to do battle. A fool draws his sword aimlessly and is prone to cut himself to death.

My tongue is my sword of power. I use it!

The dog is sometimes smarter than the owner –
Yoruba proverb

The tongue has no mind of its own. Like a dog, the tongue follows where the owner leads. If the owner leads the dog into harms' way, the dog will not question the direction or intent. The same is true for the tongue. Unlike the dog, however, the tongue has a power the owner may not always be aware of. The tongue can create. The intent of the mind creates a force for the tongue. The power of this force will materialize as a physical condition or an emotional state for the owner. The tongue knows, even when the owner forgets, what you say is what you get, whether you want it or not.

I speak with a conscious tongue.

"Doing Time"

Freedom to me, is not being locked up where I have time limits for everything, being in shackles, being escorted some places, and pat searched down whenever and wherever. Freedom to me is not having a time-limit on the phones to talk to my family and friends, waiting for someone to give me my mail, having someone monitor my every moves, my money, email, phone calls, mail, etc..... Freedom means being liberated, and not being confined to all the above things I just mentioned. Freedom looks like a world outside of these bar-wired fences, you can move around where ever you want to on your own, you don't have a time limit for this or that, there are no boundary lines you can't go over, you don't have to share a room with nobody, if you don't want to, there is no limit on what you buy from the store or how much property you can have.

"Many people will walk in and out of your life, but only true friends will leave footprints in your heart." Eleanor Roosevelt.

I discovered that when I was out there in the world, I had so many friends, some for different purposes than others, but I knew I could call them, if I just needed to chat (you know kick the bobo with). I knew who to call for a show or play, a movie or recreational activity. I remember even thinking of these so-called friends on their birthdays, special holidays and Christmases, because they were so special to me. I remember how, when each one of them had hit rock bottom, at a time in their life and when they called me, I was there for them with bells on, but sadly, it had to take me coming to prison to discover that none of them were my friends to begin with. I thought they would be standers, but instead they turned out to be nothing but "runners" and the strangest thing of all, people that I just spoke to here and there, only briefly in passing, are the ones' standing by my side now instead, holding my hands, comforting me and encouraging me, sending me cards, letters and money, these are the people, I can call my friends now, and that have left their footprints in my heart, until I leave this world!!!

"Is there a best thing about prison?"

The best thing I would have to say is you have a chance to examine yourself. And chance to look at where you went wrong and to make adjustments. I needed time to think (but hell not that long); (LOL). Sit back and really, really establish where I went wrong and how I needed to change it and what would be best for me to move forward and plan, plot, strategize and prepare. All the things I said, I'd deal with later. In prison, you have the opportunity to do all those things, to read all those books, you wanted to read, to get yourself in shape. Go back to school. You aren't doing anything else, so what's your excuse? No appointments to prepare for, no promises to keep and tomorrow's calendar page is wide open.

Think of it as a place of training and correction and it's not so bad. You also learn how to wait on God.

In prison, I was required to be more resilient, the frustrations that ate away at me, while I was sitting and waiting …. now I got my time to speak with you reading my book right now!!!

Definitions

Angels – A spirt who tells people God's Word and who is God's helper.

Anoint – To pour olive oil on a person's head. It means that God's spirit is helping that person do a special job. (NIV Bible)

Miracle – Any great show of power that goes beyond the usual laws of nature. God's miracles are wonderful signs of his power to make things right.

Faith – is designed by God to change things. It's made to move mountains, bring God's promises to pass and to bring you Victory.

Victory---Final and complete; Supremacy or superiority in battle or war;

Success in any contest or struggle involving the defeat of an opponent or

the overcoming of obstacles.

Isaiah 43:1-4

Don't be afraid. I've redeemed you. I've called your name (Mozella). You're mine. When you're in over your head, I'll be there with you. When you're in rough waters, you will not go down. When you're between a rock and a hard place, it won't be a dead end, because I am God, your personal God (Mozella). I paid a huge price for you. That's how much you mean to me! That's how much I love you!

Thank you Jesus again for delivering me out of the mire and not letting me sink, in the deep waters.

"MY GOD IS AWESOME"!!

"FINAL WORD"

Call upon me in the day of trouble. I will deliver you and you shall glorify me. (Psalm 50:15).

I was obedient, God kept his promises, and praise God, I'm glorifying him right now, with my book, that you just finished reading as my testimony. Praise God, Hallelujah!!

PRAYER FOR COURT

I pray that everything that lies in secret shall be revealed (Daniel 2:22 and Luke 8:17). Lord Jesus, I'm standing on your Word without wavering. I have made up my mind to believe the Word, no matter what I see, feel or think, regardless of what the circumstances look like, the Word of God is still alive and true and (Psalm 119:105) says your Word is a lamp to my feet and a light to my path.

Heavenly Father, you are King of Kings and the Lord of Lords. God you have promised to take care of me and deliver me, just as you did the children of Israel in the wilderness. Father God, I am also leaning on (Deuteronomy 31:8) when Moses said to Joshua, "It is the Lord who goes before you. He will be with you. He will not fail you or forsake you, and do not fear or be dismayed." In the name of Jesus, I pray and let your will be done in me (Amen) and Thank you in advance for the Victory fourth coming.

Prayer: Rescue me from my enemies, O God.

Protect me from those who come to destroy me.

Prayers for when you're waiting on the outcome of your case (Victory) to be settled in the Courtroom

Psalm 13:1-6; Psalm 27:7; Psalm 27:12-14; Psalm 31:14-18; Psalm 34:7-8; Psalm 34:15; Psalm 35:1-28; Psalm 38:15-18; Psalm 38:21-22: Psalm 39:7-8; Psalm 39:12-13; Psalm 40:14; Psalm 43:1; Psalm 46:10; Psalm 51:1-3; Psalm 56:1-5; Psalm 59:1 and 9; Psalm 69:14-18; Psalm 69:30 and 32; Psalm 86:1-7; Psalm 91:1-16; Psalm 94:1-4; Psalm 140:1-13; Psalm 141:1-2; Psalm 142:5-7; Psalm 1 - 12;

After your victory is won in Court. Psalm 145:1-21 and Psalm 146:1-10

I pray that all things you ask for, you will receive. Don't lose hope in God, there's power in prayer plus faith, and the time is now to walk on that faith. Don't give up! Keep your head above water, even if you have to doggy paddle to make it. Additionally, time spent waiting on God is never wasted.

Prayer: Please, Lord rescue me! Come quickly, Lord and help me.

Hope in the midst of the storm

Psalm 138:7 - Though I walk in the midst of trouble, you preserve my life; you stretch out your hand against the wrath of my enemies, and your right hand delivers me

Hebrews 6:19 - We have this as a sure and steadfast anchor of the soul, a hope that enters into the inner place behind the curtain,

Jesus is our lifeline and our hope. We can rely on him because he keeps us steady and productive, no matter what the circumstances may bring you. When the "2014" year came to an end, which was also my Birthday, the 31st, I had hoped and prayed that I would be home to bring in the New Years! When it didn't happen, all I could say to God, was that it wasn't in your will for me, and that I must accept. I know God that you order our steps according to Psalm 37:23. But, how many more Birthdays Lord, am I going to be here, before you set me free?

Thank you father, for giving us Jesus, as our anchor and our hope. Also, while still down on my knees, I thanked him for blessing me to see 49 years in good health and alive, because a lot of people didn't make it to see these many years. As you well know Lord, it was a crazy year while here, Thank God, you didn't take your eyes off of me for one second, or I perhaps would have perished in prison. But, thankfully again you had anointed me, therefore the spirit of the Lord was upon me, and that anointing abided in me.

God's Road - For Me!

Sometimes in our lives we want to say, "God, what's going on?" That's what I said in 2009, when I was convicted of second degree murder, while armed.

Back in the day, if someone had ever come to me, and say to me, that one day I would be in prison for this, I would have told them that they were out of their damn mind!

But, in the book of Exodus, we read that when the children of Israel left Egypt, God did not lead them on the shortest or easiest route. He did not take them on the road everyone else would have taken.

God took the Israelites on the route that would benefit them the most. (Exodus 13:17-18). He took them on the route that would prepare them for the Promised Land. Likewise, looking back now, I see that going to prison turned out to be a blessing for me, because I was able to advance my educational level higher. I would have wanted to while on the streets, but never seemed to quite get here, because I was a single mom, raising two daughters, and always the primary bread-holder in the household.

You see, God's road may not be the one we want to take. It may not be the easiest. But, it's the road he has chosen to get us to our destination successfully.

It's great to have an education and to have some idea of where we want to go in life and what we want to do. I believe God wants us to understand the road in front of us. But as opportunities come our way, we need to pray and read the Word- Our road map – to find out if that's the road God wants us to go down at that particular time.

There are many roads we can travel. But God wants us to travel on his road of blessing. He wants us to travel on his road of faith, trust, healing, strength and love. When we do, we will reach our destiny!

Remember that God is on your side and he will guide you as you travel his road for you! No testing has overtaken you that is not common to everyone. God is faithful and He will not let you be tested beyond your strength, but with the testing, he will also provide the way out to escape, so that you may be able to endure it. (1 Corinthians 10;13). And, as a result, the trials we endure can bring us closer to God.

Perhaps "Kerry" you were reading this book over my shoulders as I wrote it. I don't know, but until we meet again, let us both rest easy and leave the profundities of life to the Author and Finisher of life – GOD. I promise you that I am deeply sorry for what I have done, and I will continue to pray that you will forever forgive me.

I dedicate this book to my grandson Keshawn Jones

Mozella is 50 years old now. She lives and resides in Washington, DC.

with her family and four beautiful grand kids. Since being back home, she loves

spending quality time with family and friends. She is a multi-tasker who enjoys

reading, writing letters to her pen-pals, movies, sight-seeing at various museums,

loves to shop and loves the outdoor nature.

If you want to contact the author, you may do so on: facebook.com/Mozella Jones or send her an email at: moekids49@yahoo.com